Craig S. Van Kirk

GHOSTS ON THE RANGE

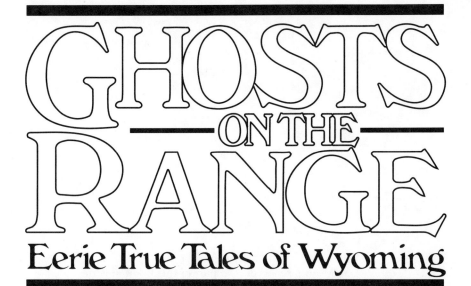

GHOSTS ON THE RANGE

Eerie True Tales of Wyoming

DEBRA D. MUNN

PRUETT PUBLISHING COMPANY
BOULDER, COLORADO

First Edition
1 2 3 4 5 6 7 8 9
Printed in the United States of America

Cover design and illustration by Byron Taylor

Munn, Debra D., 1953–
   Ghosts on the range : eerie true tales of Wyoming / Debra D.
Munn.
      p.   cm.
   Includes bibliographical references.
   ISBN 0-87108-771-5
   1. Ghosts—Wyoming.   I. Title.
BF1472.U6M85   1989
133.1'09787—dc20   89-39754
                                                              CIP

To my husband, Scott Foll,
who doesn't believe in ghosts,
but who, fortunately, believes in me.

ACKNOWLEDGMENTS

I am greatly indebted to everyone who shared their Wyoming ghost tales with me, and in addition, I would like to thank the many newspapers and magazines that ran my letters and articles asking for stories. The following people and organizations were also indispensable in helping me to put this book together.

Elaine Abrahams
Mike Badger
Angela Ballard
Gladys Beery
Don Bell
Doris Belston
Brett Boreing
Naomi Briggs
Val Brinkerhoff
Delbert Burrell
Elsa Spear Byron
Carole Cartwright
Katherine Christiansen
Mary Cleary
Cloud Peak Realty, Sheridan
Charles and Glada Clough
Daryl Coats
Cowboy Hall of Fame
Cowgirl Hall of Fame
Alpha Davis
Jim and Jo Davis
Terry Davis
Sgt. Tracy Deaton

Bill Dobbs
Tim and Peggy Dreas
Rosalie A. Eaton
Paul Fees
Georgetta Flyr
Sandy Cameron Folkerts
Fort Laramie National Historic
  Site
Marge Frazier
Mary Elizabeth Galvan
Mary Ellen Garza
Hila Gilbert
Clyde Goss
Susan Granquist
Gene M. Gressley
Janell Hanson
Gladys Heasler
Ric Heasler
Larry Higby
Bobbie Holder
Harold Hopkinson
George Horse Capture
Tom Howard

Deborah Iverson
Deb Jacobson
Marie Jacobson
Mary Lois Jacobson
Susan Johnstone
Loren K. Jost
Captain Liz Lane-Johnson
Dyfrig Lange
Edie Lawrence
Pat Litton
Janice M. Lubbers
Brenda Lynn
Gary Lynn
Carol Martin
Jerri Burroughs Martinez
Howard McEachron
Zelda McEachron
Elaine B. Moncur
Bev Moody
Jan Moore
Maurine Moore
Earl Murray
Jessica Mydland
Art Myers
Patty Myers
Rex Nebel
Julie Ottaway
J.S. Palen
June Pipkin
Peg Poague
Jinx Putnam
Robert Roten
Lesley Spahr Russell
Helen Salisbury
Sheridan County Fulmer Public
    Library

Ted Schnell
John McK. Schreiber
Annie Skidgel
Lylas Skovgard
Ant Smith
Steve Smith
Ellen Snell
Sydney Snell
Vivian Snell
Roberta Souders
Sgt. D.G. Sprong
Fiona Stalking Moon
Vashti Stevens
Cindy Taylor
June Taylor
Mike Taylor
Jo Ellen Thurlow
Richard Thurlow
University of Wyoming Library
F.E. Warren Air Force Base
Patty Way
Ron Wilcock
Richard Wilson
Jo Winkel
Wyoming Oral History Folklore
    Association
Wyoming State Archives,
    Museums, & Historical
    Department
Wyoming State Historical
    Research and Publication
    Division
Henry Yaple

CONTENTS

INTRODUCTION

W hoever heard of ghosts in Wyoming? There is a widely held prejudice that the Cowboy State, with so few citizens and even fewer Gothic mansions, just doesn't have what it takes to produce any decent spooks. But after spending three and a half years collecting tales of the supernatural from people all over Wyoming, I can attest that there are enough strange phenomena here to fill a state the size of Texas.

Within these pages, the most discriminating aficionados of the paranormal will find much to delight them—from a library built over a graveyard to a disappearing restaurant, from a museum cursed by the possession of a skull to a trailer haunted by feuding in-laws, from mischievous poltergeists to vanishing ladies in gray. In the course of preparing this book, I interviewed one hundred thirty-seven people, and I searched through books, magazines, newspapers, and files of historical societies for written information on Wyoming ghosts. Each story has been researched as completely as possible, and I have used real names of interviewees wherever I could. In those cases where my contacts requested anonymity to protect their privacy, I have given them a pseudonym, identified with an asterisk (*) the first time the name is used.

Readers are bound to notice that some of the same phenomena keep popping up in different chapters. Manifestations such as phantom footsteps, rocking chairs that rock by themselves, doors opening and closing with the help of no visible agent, malfunctions of machines and electrical devices, and other displays of psychic energy are common not only to Wyoming ghost stories, but to those from all over the world. Writers of fictional accounts of the paranormal would refrain from describing the same types of incidents again and again, but the author of reportedly true tales has no such right. The repetition of these common elements, in fact, only serves as evidence that the so-called "supernatural" world really exists and that it operates according to its own consistent body of laws, just as the "natural" world does.

F.W.H. Myers, one of the nineteenth-century founders of the Society for Psychical Research in Great Britain, claimed that "Whatever else, indeed, a 'ghost' may be, it is probably one of the most complex phenomena in nature." Over one hundred years later, we have made but few inroads in our understanding of this puzzling subject, but serious researchers have developed theories that may provide some answers.

First, although folklore around the world insists that ghosts are spirits of the dead, this is certainly not true in all cases. Many apparitions of the living have also been seen, and one such account is given in this book (see "The Doppelganger.") It is also commonly believed now that poltergeist activity (which bears practically no resemblance at all to the way it has been depicted in recent movies) is usually caused by unconscious, uncontrollable psychic energy of a living person, often an adolescent.

Along this same line, parapsychologists have come to believe that some ghosts may not be active intelligences at all, but rather impressions that have been somehow recorded upon their physical environment during a time of crisis or heightened emotions, good or bad. If that is true, these hauntings are like tape recorded material that is available for playback under the appropriate (although still not understood) conditions. This theory would account not only for the sighting of some apparitions that appear over and over in the same locale, but also for ghostly noises or even phantom odors.

Theories aside, however, ghost stories should entertain and delight; and because I tend to like all of them, one of my hardest tasks in putting this collection together was to decide which to omit. I finally decided that unless I was able to uncover new information, I would not include tales that had previously been published in other sources. But to anyone interested in Wyoming ghosts, I enthusiastically recommend the materials that appear in the Additional Readings section at the end of this book.

These previously published accounts, like the chapters in this book, are all touted as true. Naturally, there is no way to "prove" a ghost story; and while I'm convinced at least of the sincerity of all the people I interviewed, readers will have to make up their own minds about the phenomena described in each chapter.

One thing certain is that we can all be fooled; we can all be so mystified by perfectly normal events that we ascribe supernatural causes to them. Some security guards at Fort Laramie, for example, were so puzzled by a door that kept coming unlocked by itself that they decided a ghost was to blame. Closer inspection revealed that the lock on the front door to the old store was expanding and contracting because of variations in temperature, and was therefore slipping out of place. (The reason why the doors to Quarters A keep opening up has *not* been determined, however, as you will see in "The Past Never Dies at Fort Laramie.")

Another good ghost story, that of a back porch haunted by the sounds of pounding and hammering, was invalidated when a loose brick was discovered rattling around as the chimney settled. The family involved seemed sadder at losing their "ghost" than relieved to find out what had been tormenting them for the past ten years! Their disappointment is similar to that experienced by a colleague of mine, Daryl Coats, who became convinced that he was watching the antics of a phantom cat, only to turn the lights on to discover that he was really seeing his mother's scarf being blown repeatedly into the air by a furnace!

Probably the best "non-ghost" story of all, however, is that told by Eula Lee Petersen about her former husband, Chris Jensen. In the early 1930s, while Chris was homesteading in a small, isolated cabin on Dugout Creek, he worked for different ranches during the day, and at night he returned home to spend the evening with his feet in the oven, reading books or conversing with one of the few other settlers in the area. One night when it was extremely cold, he happened to glance up at the frost-coated window, and to his horror, all he could see were two large, steaming balls.

He sat there for a while longer, trying to believe his eyes. At times, smoke appeared to be flying from the strange objects, which remained pressed against the panes. For all Chris knew, it might have been the devil himself standing on the other side of that window! Finally, unable to endure the suspense any longer, he grabbed his pistol, screwed up his courage, and threw open the door as hard as he could.

"What do you want?" he demanded, trying to sound more threatening than he felt.

He received no answer, however, for standing there was not the devil incarnate that he had feared, but one of his employer's big bulls that Chris had brought back with him and then forgotten. The large steaming balls pressed against the window had been nothing more than the animal's nostrils!

Fortunately for those of us who enjoy tales of the supernatural, not all Wyoming ghost stories can be explained away that easily. So fix yourself a cup of hot cocoa, settle down into a comfortable chair, and enjoy!

THE HAUNTING
OF THE
BYRON SCHOOL

I t's not unusual for schools to have the reputation of being haunted. Young people everywhere are quick to invent tales of headless goblins lurking about the hallways, or bloodthirsty ghouls lying in wait in the cafeteria— anything to spice up the daily routine. But the stories surrounding Byron's consolidated Elementary and. Rocky Mountain High School are told not only by students who have watched too many horror movies; some of the most spine-tingling tales come from those who work there, ranging from custodians to superintendents.

Several janitors have had strange experiences in the building. About ten years ago, Janis Adams* had gone upstairs to fetch some cleaning supplies when she became aware of a sudden, intense feeling of cold, and an overpowering, horrible smell that she isn't able to describe. "I knew that it wasn't anything to do with the cleaning supplies," she said. "But I couldn't move, and I felt as though I couldn't scream, either. In my mind, I said a quick prayer, and then I noticed something that looked like smoke moving away from me as a whirlwind might. I ran down the stairs, and at the foot I met the maintenance man, who told me, 'You look like you've seen a ghost!' And I said, 'I saw something, and I'm scared to death.' I told him that I would never go up there alone again, and I haven't. I'd never had an experience like that before. For some reason, I knew I wasn't alone."

Another custodian, Eddie Davis, was cleaning the inside windows of one of the elementary classrooms five or six summers ago when behind him, he heard a clicking noise. "I looked around, but I couldn't see anything, so I continued working. I heard the noise again and looked around, when I noticed that the sound was coming from a small adding machine. The third time I heard it, I went over to investigate, and I found that the adding machine wasn't even plugged in! But that definitely seemed to be where the noise was coming from."

Similar unexplained noises from office equipment have long been reported in the old school, and they are apparently still occurring. One of the most commonly affected rooms is the old art room, which is now used for weight training. Donna Weathermon, who was a student in the 1960s and '70s, and who often cleaned up after school functions, frequently heard the sounds of someone typing furiously in the weight room.

"You would swear you heard a typewriter going clickety clickety click up there, just as loud and clear as if you were in the room next door," she explained. "I've talked to a lot of people who have heard the same thing. And once in a while you could hear what sounded like someone walking around when no one was there."

More recently, during cheerleading tryouts in the spring of 1988, a group of girls was practicing late one night in the wrestling room, which is right above the weight room. "All the cheerleaders had gone home except for three of us, and the only other people in the school were the janitors, who were all on the first floor," remembered JLee Van Grinsven of the class of 1992. "The lights in the weight room were turned off and the door was locked. But we kept hearing the sounds of weights clinking and clanking below us. There's a hole in the wrestling room floor that lets you see into the weight room, and when we looked into it, we saw that the lights were all off, but we could still hear the sounds of the weights dropping. We heard them even when we were going down the stairs to leave for the evening, although the door remained locked and the lights were still off."

Alan Bair, who was superintendent during most of the 1970s and early '80s, was working in his office one evening after dark, while a group of students was decorating the building for an upcoming dance. "Suddenly there was a disturbance out in the hall, and students came into my office to report that they had heard a noise up where the ghost was supposed to be," he said. "That place was up a narrow stairway in the older part of the building, and blocking the stairs was a metal collapsible gate that was latched on the opposite wall to prevent people from going back and forth. The students wanted the key to go up, so I followed them to the bottom of the stairway, where we all stood in a huddle to listen. After a while, we heard the noise, which could best be described as something between a rattling and a scuffing. It was intermittent, happening every two or three minutes.

"We devised a plan to split into pairs and search the school, but nobody found anything. After we drifted back together, we just sat quietly and waited for the noise to reappear, but it never did. I personally don't think there's a ghost; I just think the strange sounds are caused by atmospheric conditions."

The most common mysterious occurrence in recent years is the turning on of lights in the weight and wrestling rooms when no one has been in the area. "Lots of times when you drive by at night, you can see those lights on inside the building," said Tracy Folkerts of the class of 1991. "One of the coaches last year would always lock up the door and turn off the lights, but if anyone came back at night, he'd find the lights on inside the room with the still-locked door."

The most convincing story that something or someone has haunted the Byron school for a long time comes from Harold Hopkinson, who was superintendent from 1952 to 1963. "This was a new job for me, and I was eager to make good," he explained. "So during my first few months at the school, I often worked late at night, going over all the books and records, so that I'd know what had gone on before and what I might expect in the future.

"One October or November evening about eight or nine o'clock, I was working in my office on the second floor. As usual, I was alone, but then I heard somebody open the front door and come up the stairway. I waited for whoever it was, and thought that the steps were heading toward the library, which was up a short flight of stairs just past my office. I watched but didn't see who it was, and I heard the steps go up into the library.

"I went out into the hall to see who had come in, but there was no one in the library or on the steps leading to it. I decided I must have imagined the footsteps, so I went back to my office to work.

"Pretty soon, the door to the library opened, and I heard someone go down the stairs. Now this time, I was quite alert, and I was watching, but I still didn't see anyone. I heard the steps go by my office, so I walked into the hall, where I heard them go down the stairs. I went to the balcony overlooking the stairs, but I saw no one on the landing. Then I heard the front door open, but I didn't see it, probably, I thought, because I hadn't gotten there fast enough.

"I was puzzled as to who it might have been, but since I was eager to get my work done, I went back into my office. And then the front doors opened again. This time, I thought that I had to find out who was playing a trick on me. So I went to the landing just as the front door banged shut, but I didn't see anyone. So I backed over towards my office, and then I heard the steps coming up the stairway. But when it seemed as if they should have been at the top of the stairs, I still didn't see anyone. I was still backing into my office when the footsteps went right in front of me! Right up the steps to the library, and then the door opened, but there was not a soul to be seen!

"Needless to say, I was frightened by now, so I went into my office and gathered up all my things; then I forced myself to go up to check the library, but as I had feared, there was no one there. I came back down and locked my office door, turned out the lights, went down the hallway, down the stairs, and out the front door. And for years I didn't go to the school again to work at night!

"Later, I mentioned my experience to a few people, but most of them thought I was joking," he continued. "In my last years as superintendent, I did go back to my office on a couple occasions at night, but I was nervous all the time I was there."

Harold Hopkinson is still baffled about what he heard that night. "It couldn't have been a person coming up the stairs, because I would have seen him. My eyesight has been pretty keen all my life, and then it was especially so. I can't explain what happened. But I did hear somebody come through the front door, up the stairs, and across the hall, which wasn't carpeted, but wood, so it made all the creaks and groans that you would expect. And the stairway up to the library was wood, too.

"The eerie thing is that if I had had my eyes shut, I would have *known* that there was somebody walking right in front of me. But my eyes were wide open and I didn't see anyone, although the back of my neck began to tingle.

"I didn't believe in ghosts before that happened, and I really don't now," he confessed. "I think it's possible that there are such things, of course, and I believe that people never really die. But I also think that a greater power wouldn't let these spirits wander around aimlessly. So if they come back, they have to have a purpose, I think."

If Harold Hopkinson is correct in his theory, what was the purpose of the spirit who repeatedly trod the stairs that evening? Or was this particular haunting caused merely by the "playing back" of impressions recorded in the environment, the wooden floor and the stairs? That may solve the case of the phantom footsteps, and perhaps even the sounds of the office machines and the clanking weights, but what causes the lights to go on for no obvious reason? And what caused Janis Adams's frightening encounter with the cold, malodorous whirlwind?

Explanations of the haunting at the Byron school range from a silly theory that a cook was once murdered there and ground into hamburger meat (doubtlessly improving the flavor of the school lunch), to the more serious suggestion espoused by many students and even some faculty that a teacher once committed suicide in what was then the art room but is now the wrestling room.

To check out the latter rumor, I talked with former superintendent Jim Simmons, who served from 1945 to 1952, and with several other oldtimers associated with the school. All of them were absolutely certain that no teacher had ever committed suicide in Byron, and they were equally sure that if one had done so, the entire town would have known about it.

Long-time Byron resident Rose Griffin Doty, however, who attended the school and then taught there in the early 1920s, was able to shed some light on how the rumor might have evolved from the confusion of two separate tragedies in the town's history.

In the 1920s, natural gas came to the residents of Byron, and before regulators were installed on the lines, there were several gas fires in homes. A victim of one of those domestic fires was a Byron teacher; and about twenty years later, in the 1940s, another man committed suicide. The latter had absolutely nothing to do with the school, however; but it is easy to see how, with the passage of time, the deaths of the two men could have fused in the public memory to create the rumor that a teacher had committed suicide in the school.

If that is not the cause of the ghostly manifestations at the Byron school, what is? No one knows, but it's a certainty that few of the town's residents like being alone in the building after dark!

THE DOPPELGANGER

W hether ghosts are actually spirits or just leftover psychic imprints from days gone by, most people associate them with the dead. But recorded history notes many apparitions of persons still living, and the most perplexing of these encounters involve the sighting of one's own double, or doppelganger, as it is called in German. Such historic personages as Goethe, Queen Elizabeth I, Percy Bysshe Shelley, and Guy de Maupassant were reported to have seen their doubles, and while such encounters are sometimes interpreted as harbingers of death, just as often they seem to benefit those who experience them.

The strange story of George Hensley* is a case in point. It begins on a cold night during World War II, when Sergeant Hensley was trying to find a warm place for himself and his squad to sleep. Because the ground never warmed up no matter how long one slept on it, the sergeant ignored General George Patton's warning posted on the door that intruders would be shot, and pushed his way into a pitch black building.

"Gee, Sarge," said a man named Maxwell. "This place is off limits. Anyway, the damn SS troops are everywhere around here." The sergeant paid him no attention, but kept feeling his way in the dark, as a light was far too dangerous to use. With his hands held out in front of him, he explored the room, which seemed to be full of huge cases reaching to the ceiling, leaning against each other with only enough room to squeeze in at the bottom.

"Let me see what's here, Sarge," whispered Maxwell. He closed the door cautiously and ducked into one of the narrow spaces. George followed him. Shielding his flashlight with one hand, Maxwell switched it onto the huge dividers, and was rewarded by the sight of voluptuous nude maidens smiling back at him, on canvasses fifteen feet high on either side. The men had stumbled into one of the cache houses used by the Nazis to store their stolen art.

"No wonder Patton is on guard!" exclaimed George. "This is perfect—we'll stay here," he said, and crawled into one of the openings. Utterly exhausted and glad to be in out of the cold, he was asleep before he hit the floor.

Later, at some point during the night, George Hensley awoke with a shock. Someone was slashing at him with an SS knife! Perhaps the German soldier had been surprised to see the place occupied. The blade came down again and again, and each time George tried to fend it off with his forearms and elbows, working them instinctively in a sort of washboard motion. His Eisenhower jacket, the khaki jacket with the knit collar and cuffs that all the World War II troops had been given, seemed to be taking the brunt of the fight, however, and the sleeves were already cut to pieces. Just then George kicked and caught something on the soldier, perhaps the SS belt, and the German slid back toward the entrance. The young sergeant then scrambled out of the cubbyhole in which he had slept and jumped out the window, then ran across a field and into some trees. Fighting to keep from breathing too loudly and thus giving away his position, he felt the arms of his jacket hanging in ribbons.

"This jacket is my lucky rabbit's foot," he thought. "I'm not going to turn this in. I'll fix it and keep on wearing it until I get out of the war."

The war ended and George Hensley was discharged from the infantry in March 1946. He returned to his family's farm near Cody; then in the fall he returned to the University of Wyoming to continue the education that had been interrupted.

George soon discovered that he needed a car in Laramie, so when spring vacation came, he returned to the ranch to pick up the used army jeep that he had purchased earlier that summer for $100. When he began his return journey to the campus at six o'clock on a freezing dark morning, he was decked out in a parka with mittens, boots, and a fur hat. The wind whistled in his ears as the open jeep lumbered at maximum speed through the badlands and cold prairies. When he reached Shoshone, the sun came up, but it furnished no warmth, only light, and he continued in the frigid wilderness all the way to Casper, where he stopped for a few hours to visit a friend.

Back on the road that afternoon, George had about two hundred fifty miles to go. The pale Wyoming sky was already darkening, and the wind whistled more fiercely than ever. George Hensley was a healthy twenty-four-year-old, but he nevertheless began to feel the effects of being too long in the cold, especially after snow began falling into his open vehicle. At one point he picked up a hitchhiking Indian, a big, strong man who never said a word until they reached a small town.

"Let me out of this damn jeep," he said. "I'm freezing!"

The snow continued falling, and George worked the jeep's manual windshield wipers with his left hand and steered with the right as he tried to keep the view clear in front of him. The lights of Wheatland finally shone ahead through the driving snow, and he stopped for coffee somewhere along the bleak, deserted main street. The sky was pitch black as he resumed his journey, and the nearer to Laramie he got, the higher the altitude and the worse the storm became.

Out of Wheatland there are two routes to Laramie, and George wanted to take the shortcut that led through twisting, sheer Telephone Canyon and eventually opened onto the Laramie plateau. The road was narrow, with no guardrails, and one side sheered off into something that resembled a black pit at night.

But George noticed something wrong. A huge Greyhound bus was stopped, and a police car blocked the turnoff into the canyon. George parked his jeep, got out, and trudged through the six inches of just fallen snow to the bus, where the driver and passengers were talking with the police.

"No one is going through that canyon tonight," announced the highway patrolman. "It's too dangerous. It's only a one-way road in places, and since there's no guardrails, with one wrong move you could end up in the canyon and nobody would find you until spring."

The bus driver accepted the information calmly, but George was going wild. If he couldn't go through the canyon, he'd have to go through Cheyenne, and that meant going fifty miles farther after being on the road for fourteen hours already.

"No way!" he thought as he climbed back into the jeep and reversed his tracks toward Wheatland. When he was a mile away but still in sight of the intersection, he turned off his lights, turned the jeep around, and waited for both the bus and the police car to drive away.

George started the jeep cautiously, and as the highway patrol car moved toward Cheyenne, he drove slowly back to the cutoff into Telephone Canyon.

By this time, George was fatigued and trying hard to stay awake. As he left the intersection and drove down to the canyon entrance, his headlights shone onto the figure of a man walking along the road toward him.

As all residents of Wyoming know, refusal to help other people who are stranded in the winter almost always leads to their certain death. But where did this man come from on a night like this, George wondered, as he pulled over to talk to him. They were fifteen miles from Wheatland, there were no ranches in sight, and nothing was visible anywhere but the white sky and the snowy prairie.

As the hitchhiker crossed the road and stood in the beam of the headlights, George noticed that he was dressed in an Eisenhower jacket, the same kind that he himself had worn in the war. The war! In a flash George was back in the darkened Nazi storehouse, with the German storm trooper above him slashing at his arms and chest. After the war, George had sewn up the tattered sleeves of his lucky Eisenhower jacket, and although the result had been none too attractive, it was his most treasured possession.

Now George recognized that same jacket with the bad stitching on the lower sleeves as his own. And as he looked more closely at the man, he saw that he, too, was uncannily familiar. He was an exact replica of himself, in fact. Perhaps from a slightly earlier time, but himself, nevertheless.

But none of this seemed to matter, since George was reaching the point of exhaustion.

"You look very tired," said the hitchhiker. "Want me to drive?"

"Great idea," George said sleepily. "I've been driving for fourteen hours."

At that, he moved over to the passenger's side and lay down between the seats, pulling his parka forward to keep his skin off the cold metal. As his head touched the floor, he snuggled down and fell asleep.

Some time later, he awoke and at first could not remember where he was, until the cold floor of the jeep reminded him. A coyote wailed somewhere in the distance, and George sat up, breathing in the cold, clean air. The jeep was stopped, the hitchhiker was sitting behind the wheel, and the welcoming lights of Laramie were visible in the distance. The two men had traveled unscathed through the treacherous Telephone Canyon.

"I feel great," George said, as he yawned and stretched. "Coming into Laramie with me?" But the question was more rhetorical than meaningful, for where else could the man go? There were no ranches nearby on this side of the canyon; only Bosler Junction lay close by, and there was nothing there.

"No, thanks, I'll get out here," replied the hitchhiker as he stepped out of the jeep.

"Well, thanks a lot!" George said. "So long!" He started the motor and the jeep lurched forward on its way again. For a while George watched the hitchhiker. He was walking back into the canyon.

George had never been so glad to get to his fraternity house. He immediately slept again for twelve hours, and spent the next day practically alone, since all roads to the university were closed, and his friends couldn't get through.

On the following day the roads had cleared, and a welcome back party was set for that evening. "Who belongs to that jeep?" someone yelled, as the keg of beer was rolled into the dining room and festivities were about to begin.

"That's mine," George said. "I brought it from the ranch."

"Must have been some rough time coming in," said his friend Basil.

"Naw," said George, "I came through Telephone Canyon and cut off about an hour."

The others took a pause from sipping their beer. "You came through Telephone Canyon?" asked Basil incredulously. "But it was blocked at both ends and snowed in in the middle. The cops wouldn't even let us try it!"

"Oh, I have four-wheel drive in that jeep," George bragged. "Anyway, I didn't have to drive it all the way; I picked up a hitchhiker at the Wheatland end. I took a nap while he drove."

Silence settled over the room, and there was another pause. "A hitchhiker in Telephone?" one of the fraternity men asked. "How did he get there?"

"I don't know," George said, "but he was there all right. And kind of lightly dressed for that weather, come to think of it." For the first time, George remembered the incident with perfect recall.

"Funny thing about him," he continued to his listeners, "he looked exactly like me. He was even wearing my old jacket."

The others looked at him aghast, as if they thought he had lost his mind.

"Aw, heck," George said to appease them. "I must have been drunk!"

This explanation may have satisfied his audience, but it didn't satisfy George, who has continued to puzzle over the encounter with his double for all these years. He now wonders whether fatigue combined perhaps with the onset of hypothermia didn't cause him to imagine the whole episode as he drove himself through Telephone Canyon. The entire incident, he admitted, did feel like a dream in which preposterous things seem perfectly ordinary. Or is it possible that, unlikely as it seems, he really did pick up a hitchhiker and then mentally transposed his own features and the Eisenhower jacket on the man? The only other solution must be that he really did encounter his own doppelganger, who had come for the sole purpose of rescuing him from a dangerous drive he would quite probably never have survived.

GHOSTS, GHOSTS
ON THE
RANGE

Some people seem to have a knack for attracting things that go bump in the night, and the family of Sam* and Ida Edwards* definitely fall into this category. Sam and Ida and their children were no strangers to psychic phenomena of all kinds, but in the early spring of 1978, they were hoping for peace and quiet when they moved from Idaho to the northwest part of Wyoming. Sam had gotten a job on a small, private ranch outside of Meeteetse, and his family were to live in the spacious house that had stood on the property for more than a hundred years.

At seven or eight o'clock on their first night, Ida was cooking flapjacks on an antique green stove while her husband, two sons, and assorted ranch hands were moving furniture and boxes into the house.

"At one point while I was cooking, I heard the truck pull out of the drive, but I didn't think that all of the men had left," Ida recalled, "because into the kitchen came this nice looking young guy in his mid-twenties, about five-ten or so. He was wearing a cowboy shirt, leather vest, jeans, a belt, and brown, scuffed boots. He wore no hat and his blond hair was thinning on top. He wiped his feet on the mat like everybody else had done, but I noticed that he made a soft, barely audible stomping sound. When he saw me, his mouth fell open and he had the most shocked expression, as if to ask, 'Who in the world are you?'

"I said, 'Hello, do you work here? Are you one of the boss's sons?' But he just stood and stared at me with his jaws agape for what seemed like five minutes. I got a little nervous and began to say things like, 'Hello, we're the Edwards, and we've just moved in here. What's your name?'

"But he never said a word, just kept staring until he finally shrugged his shoulders, turned around, and walked back out the door. I decided that maybe he was hard of hearing or had some kind of emotional problem. Through the window, I watched him walk part of the way down the path in front of the house, where a big light had been turned on.

"Almost at the same time, the others came back, and I began asking them about the guy who had just been in the kitchen. They kept insisting that nobody else had been on the premises, and that they had all gone off in the pickup and had just returned.

"I told Sam that he had to have seen him, that the two of them must have been close enough to brush elbows when they passed each other on the walkway. After all, there had been only a few seconds between the time when the young man left the house and the others came up the path.

"Finally I convinced them that I had seen *someone*, so we went outside and looked around, but there were no signs of anybody. We even looked for footprints, but there were none except for those belonging to our own family. And the prints were distinct and easy to see, because it was so wet and muddy that everyone had carefully stepped back into his own so as not to make more of a mess.

"I got to thinking," Ida continued, "how everyone but this fellow had cast a shadow as he walked by the light out in front. And it was also odd that the dogs didn't bark, as they usually do whenever there's a stranger around. So, half jokingly, I told my family that I had seen a ghost."

About ten days later, the Edwards's seventeen-year-old son Andy* was able to corroborate his mother's story. After he had finished stacking hay in the barn, he came into the house and mentioned that he, too, had seen the mystery man.

"Andy said that the same man had been out in the barn, sitting on top of a bale of hay. He even showed Andy a better way to stack the hay, by directing with his hands where to put each bale and how to push it into place. Andy said that he looked just the way I had described him, except that he was transparent!

"The old man who owned the ranch came over a couple days later, looked in the barn, and said, 'Hey, somebody around here knows how to stack hay! That's exactly the way I would have done it, and I've never had anyone do it right before!'"

The next ghostly sighting occurred one afternoon when Sam Edwards was repairing a replica of a small, 1910, one-horse delivery wagon. Because the wagon had always been kept clean and was often used for special occasions such as weddings, the Edwards hesitated to store it in the dirty barn, so it was kept inside as a kind of storage bin.

"Sam was lying underneath the wagon to repair the running gear, and I was in a room close by," Ida remembered. "All at once, he gasped and I heard a loud bump as he banged his head on the underside of the wagon. I ran to see what was the matter, and there sat my husband with a startled look on his face, his mouth open and his eyes big as saucers. He said, 'A woman just came floating by me!'

"He said that she was attractive, had brown hair, appeared to be about twenty-five years old, and was wearing a long and heavy, beige-colored muslin nightgown. He said she walked in through one wall, smiled and nodded, her mouth moving as though she were greeting him, but he didn't hear any sound. And then she floated about a foot and a half over his chest and right on through the other wall. He said that like the young man Andy had seen, this woman was transparent, and Sam had the feeling that she might have been the male ghost's wife.

"I asked him if she had touched him, and he said no. In fact, he said, he had looked up under the gown as it floated past him, and he could see her bare feet, even her toenails, but above them the gown was empty—no legs, no underclothing—it was just like looking into a tent. That's when he bumped his head, when the shock of seeing her forced him out from under the wagon. He came up so fast that he lifted the whole thing up!"

After this incident, the Edwards began hearing the unexplainable sounds of a tea party taking place in the living room.

"If you were in the hallway and the living room door was open, you'd hear the sounds softly; but if the door was closed, the sounds were loud, and you could almost make out words," Ida explained. "And you could hear laughter, along with teacups and glasses clinking. All of us heard it. But as soon as you opened the door, no matter how quickly, there was always dead silence. Then, oddly enough, if you closed the door again and stood in the living room, the sounds would continue in the hall. And if you closed the hall off, you could hear the sounds up the stairs!"

Other events reinforced the belief that the Edwards were not alone in their house. "Lots of times, we went to get groceries in town at night, and when we came home, we would see lights on upstairs, even though we were always careful to turn them off when we left. But often, as we drove close enough for headlight beams to shine inside, the lights would suddenly blink out. And of course, there was never anyone there. The old man who owned the ranch kept griping about the way we were driving up his electric bill, and we never could convince him that we weren't the ones leaving the lights on."

Ida also said that over and over again, she had the feeling she was being watched, and quite often she heard the unmistakable sounds of a child running and slamming himself against the walls upstairs.

"The commotion was so great that the whole house would shake, and you could see dust sifting through from overhead. And I would say time and again, 'Andy, get your little brother out of there. I just cleaned upstairs!' And sometimes my son Clint* *would* be playing up there, but more often than not, Andy would just point out the window and tell me, 'Save your breath, Mom. Clint's right there, playing outside!'

"Sometimes, when things started banging around like that, I played the piano," Ida said. "I knew a lot of old-fashioned tunes which apparently cast a spell over the spooks, because it would be fifteen or twenty minutes before the noises started up again."

But even with Ida's attempts to soothe the spirits, the atmosphere in the house was far from inviting. As a result, no one wanted to sleep there, so the family spent their nights in the trailer they had brought with them.

"We also made it a rule at night not to leave anyone alone in the house," Ida explained. "One bright moonlit evening I was writing a letter to my mother, and Andy was sitting up with me, drumming his fingers on the table, impatient to go to bed. Suddenly he gasped, and I looked up to see a nightgown floating in front of the window outside the house. It was filled out with the contours of a female body, and it was moving as if somebody were walking, about four feet off the ground. But there was nobody in it. I felt sure it was the same nightgown that Sam had seen the young woman wearing. I dropped my pen, and Andy stuttered, 'M-m-mother, let's get out of here!' I grabbed the letter to finish it the next day, and we ran out of the house and into the trailer as fast as we could."

After living on the ranch for only a month, the Edwards decided that they couldn't stand much more. They became especially worried when things inside their trailer began moving mysteriously from place to place. Sam found a job at another ranch near Buffalo and gave the old man his two-week notice.

"In spite of all the trouble we'd had with him, the boss was very upset at our leaving," Ida said. "We dropped subtle hints about why we were going, but that just made him clam up. We knew that he was aware of the strange occurrences in the house, but he obviously didn't want to talk about them."

The day of departure drew nearer, and once again Ida heard mysterious sounds upstairs. "There was the bang, bang, thud, thud, as if Clint were running around up there," she said. "These were thundering footsteps that made the whole top floor creak, and dust was filtering down, getting my newly cleaned house all dirty. I told Andy to go upstairs to get his brother, when he calmly pointed out the window to where Clint was playing.

" 'I don't know what to do,' I said in exasperation, and just then, we heard the bed upstairs being pulled out from the wall.

"I told Andy that we were going up there to find out what was happening, but neither of us wanted to go first. We ended up wrapping our arms around each other's waist to walk up the stairs together. When we got to the room in question, we flung open the door to dead silence. But the bed had been moved out about a foot and a half from the wall. I looked at Andy and said, 'That does it! Let's pack right now. I refuse to stay here another day!'

"I called the new boss and said we were coming early, using the excuse that my husband and his employer weren't getting along too well. And then we took off as soon as we got the rest of our stuff loaded up."

Among the household goods the Edwards took was a set of four chairs and a table that the boss had given them in gratitude for sprucing up the house. They were of a 1920s vintage, and when cleaned and dyed, they had been an attractive addition to the dining room. Inside the house, they had caused no problems, but once the Edwards left the ranch with them, an incredible series of events occurred.

Only seven or eight miles down the road, Sam's pickup developed a glitch and needed repairs. A little farther on, Andy's truck broke down and had to be hauled away to be fixed, which took most of the afternoon. On the road again, just as they were going over the pass on the way from Meeteetse to Sheridan, Ida's car blew a tire.

"Suddenly I was hanging eighteen inches over the edge of a cliff, looking down into a lake with hard ice!" Ida explained. "Then, when we came into the next little town, Sam's truck broke down again. To make a long story short, we had three more tires go flat, and each time we had to stop to fix and put them back on. Andy's truck broke down three more times, and the last time we had to leave it until his dad could come back for it. And as he was driving down a steep pass into Buffalo, Sam suddenly lost the brakes on the house trailer, and down he went, screaming into his CB. A man traveling behind him told him to stick with the rig until he got to the truck ramp, and that's what he did, even though at first he had been tempted to jump out and abandon the whole shebang. So up the ramp he went, scraping out the highest and biggest ruts the police had ever seen! They must have been three feet deep.

"Well, that did it! Sam said, 'Let's throw that set of table and chairs out!' But I was afraid that doing so might anger the spirits even more. So I said, 'Let's wait. I know one way to get out of this. We're going to give those things to God!'

"So we found a secondhand, Salvation Army type of store, and gave the owner the furniture, with the warning that it was haunted. He said that was no problem, and eventually a lovely couple bought the whole set for thirty-five dollars, even though they, too, had been warned. And immediately all our bad luck stopped.

"I still can't figure out what happened, though," Ida mused. "Was somebody mad because we took the table and chairs? I mean, they had been given to us, but maybe the spirits thought they belonged to the ranch. And we never did find out what caused the haunting of the house, although there was talk in town that it might have been the site of a massacre, in which a husband, wife, and seven children were killed. There was also a rumor that someone had died in the upstairs room where we found the bed moved out from the wall. But we were never sure that any of this was true."

The one thing the family *were* sure about was that they were tired of spooks and glad to move on to another locale. But because the Edwards attract the supernatural the way other people attract stray cats, they soon found themselves plagued with a brand new cast of ghostly characters. But as the saying goes, that's another story.

THE HAUNTED TRAILER

Everybody has heard of a haunted house, but how many have ever heard of a haunted trailer?

Certainly Dolly Larson of Cody had never imagined such a thing until the death of her husband, Roy, in November 1982. Her mother, who had lived with the couple for a short time, had died in 1977, so after Roy's death, Dolly was left to live in the trailer by herself.

Or so she thought. But Roy and Dolly's mother Bea had never gotten along very well in life, and it seemed to Dolly that they intended to resume their battle in the afterlife, as well.

"When my mother died, there were no problems," Dolly explained. "But then, right after my husband died, it seemed like the two of them got back together again in this trailer. For a good year afterwards, things used to happen every night.

"I'd hear walking in this house. Someone would just walk, walk, walk, up and down the hall, especially at night. And I heard what sounded exactly like their two sets of footsteps in this back room that they both occupied. Because it was Mother's room first when she was ill, and then it was his room. And I call it their room yet. I don't even go back in there!" Dolly insisted.

Her cousin Kelly Hall stayed in this room on a two-week visit in August 1984, and she was constantly troubled by strange phenomena.

"Almost every night, shortly after I'd turn off the light, I would start to hear knocking," Kelly explained. "The first night, I thought that probably the panelling in the mobile home was cooling off and crackling. But then I realized that the noise was coming not from the walls, but from an outside door in the hallway leading from my room. I wanted to make sure that nobody was outside trying to get in, so I got up and looked around."

The night in question was stifling and hot, without a hint of breeze, Kelly remembered. And yet, when she looked at the open window near the door, its flimsy curtain was puffed almost straight out, as if a strong wind were blowing. And all the time, the tapping noises continued.

"I noticed that the raps were moving gradually into my bedroom. The sounds seemed to be localized into one spot, but that spot traveled all around the room. It wasn't as if I'd hear it in one corner one time and on another wall the next. It was just as if you had someone in your room who was knocking on the paneling and systematically moving around the room. And it sounded like more than one person knocking, too. I heard the noises for what seemed like hours, but I finally went to sleep," Kelly said.

"Dolly had mentioned in passing that she still felt the presence of her mother and husband, so the next morning I told her I had heard something awfully strange and I was just wondering if it could have been Roy and my Auntie Bea. She took it all in stride, laughed, and said that it probably was. But I got a little worried—I just don't like sleeping in the same room with a bunch of ghosts!" Kelly said.

"Because this was going on almost every night, I was afraid to go to sleep, and I wasn't getting enough rest," she continued. "It was the same pattern all the time, except the noises didn't always start in the hall. Quite often they would start right in my room. After a couple nights I complained again to Dolly, and she told me that the spirits were aware of my presence and wanted to see what I was doing in their room."

One night, Dolly heard the noises herself and came to check whether they were bothering Kelly.

"I went in, put some lights on, and told her, 'Look, there's nobody here!'" remembered Dolly. "The room was completely empty, of course. But then, to reassure her, I called out to the room, 'Mother and Roy both, I want you to listen to me! You're scaring the heck out of Kelly. It's just Kelly; you remember her. You two behave yourselves and leave her alone!' "

Apparently the ghosts paid attention, since they were quiet for the rest of that night. But mischievous spirits are hard to subdue for long, and soon Kelly was again victim to the nightly routine.

"One night I was really fed up and jittery, besides being wide-eyed from lack of sleep," she said. "I didn't want to bother Dolly, of course, so I got up and went into the living room to sleep on the couch. There's only a serving bar between that room and the kitchen, so together they make one large area.

"Well, I'll be darned if there weren't noises in the cabinets! It was just light enough with the moonlight that I could see that nothing was being disturbed, but it sounded just like the cabinet doors were being opened and shut! Finally Dolly realized that I was up, and she said, 'It isn't going to do you any good to go out there. I hear them in the kitchen a lot.' "

Dolly added that such havoc was far from unusual, and that the cupboards and the refrigerator door often did actually open and close by themselves. "The back door would even open by itself sometimes, and I'd find it left that way, even though I knew I had locked it."

Another time, Kelly remembers that Dolly was showing her some clothes when she suddenly stopped to exclaim, "Mother, dammit, get out of my closet!" Dolly said that she had seen her clothes rippling, even though there was not a breath of air stirring. Dolly explained to her cousin, "Mother's fingering around in my clothes, wanting to see what I've got there. You know, she always was so darned nosy!"

Another visitor, Dolly's husband's niece from Portland, Oregon, was left alone by the troublesome spirits. "She came here and slept," Dolly said, "and I warned her about what had been going on. But she just told me, 'Oh, that doesn't bother me. My husband has also just passed away and I'm used to having him in my house looking after me, even though he's gone.' So she slept back there and nothing bothered her one bit!"

What did bother Dolly, however, were the battles that the two ghosts sometimes fought in the living room.

"Sometimes my mother and Roy really got to fighting and they hauled furniture around. I've never seen anything actually being moved, but you could come out here and turn the lights on, and sometimes the chairs and sofa would be pushed into the middle of the floor!

"I think they were still just fighting over me, over attention they didn't get. Because in life, if I'd give one attention, the other would be jealous—oh, it was terrible! They always tore me between them; you know, like a pulley," Dolly said and laughed.

"All this went on for a good year or better after Roy died; then I took a trip to California and left them to fight it out without me. Evidently, they couldn't follow me, and when I got back, their visits were more spasmodic. They seemed to have subdued their behavior a little bit.

"And now I think they've either gotten to be friends or buried the hatchet and decided to make the best of it. Once in awhile, I'll hear only one set of footsteps, and I think they're my husband's, because they're heavier. And sometimes, I think they're both together again, but they don't stay, and my husband doesn't seem to walk in the living room like he used to. The whole thing seems to be dissipating.

"Sometimes even now, though, Roy's chair will seem to be rocking by itself and I'll think that he's watching TV with me like he used to. And I have felt him riding in the car with me a lot. In fact, I'm sure he rode home with me from Sheridan right after he died. I just knew he was in that car with me. And then when I went out to Bonanza to eat one night, why, I was sitting there having my hamburger and all of a sudden, somebody's foot was on mine, rubbing it. And I could just tell it was him! Just like I know that it's both Roy and my mother who haunted this trailer together. I couldn't tell you how I know, except that I just felt it, and I recognized their footsteps.

"And the cat can always tell when they are here. He'll stand up right on his hind legs, and his eyes get real big and round. The other cat I had was even more sensitive to their presence. His eyes would get huge and his tail would fluff out—you couldn't keep him inside this trailer!" Dolly said.

"I had never even thought much about the supernatural until all this happened, and at first it bothered me. You don't think about it until it happens to you, and it's a little weird at first. And yet I knew that nobody was trying to hurt me. But once when I heard them, before I really got used to having them around again, I sat up in bed and hollered out, 'For crying out loud, be quiet!' Then I'd make myself go back to sleep.

"But now they don't stay like they used to," Dolly admits, maybe a trifle wistfully. "Mama hasn't come back much at all, but Roy's still here once in awhile. But at least there's no more moving furniture; there's no more of this nonsense of slamming cupboards and opening doors. They don't do anything to scare me anymore."

THE RESTAURANT
THAT
DISAPPEARED

O ne of the most baffling supernatural phenomena ever to take place in Wyoming occurred in March 1959. Bob Wetzel* was stationed at Lowry Air Force Base in Denver, Colorado, and he and friends John and Dee Greeley* were driving up to visit Bob's wife Sharon, who was living in Worland.

Just as the three were leaving the Cheyenne city limits, a blinding spring snowstorm hit. Whereas it normally took only a short time to get from Cheyenne to Chugwater, this trip through the blizzard took an hour and a half. Road conditions kept getting worse and worse, and anyone who has ever traveled on Wyoming highways can appreciate the relief the travelers felt when they were finally able to make out the dim, beckoning lights of a restaurant in the distance.

"We were so glad to find a place to come in out of the storm and have dinner," Bob said. "We pulled off to the left side of the road and walked across the street; then we ran up some steps leading into the building. I believe that we went through some swinging doors there in the front, and I remember that we were the only three having dinner at the time. The help were there—the cook, dishwasher, and others—but we were the only customers.

"The restaurant was quite pleasant, with white linen tablecloths, silverware, and tall water glasses at each place setting. Two young women dressed in long white dresses with black and white aprons waited on us, and to the best of my recollection, John and I both had steaks and Dee had chicken. Each of us also had a beer. When we finished our meal, we were very surprised to see the tab on our bill—it came to only nine dollars for the three of us! I was so pleased that I left five one dollar bills as a tip, and you should have seen how surprised the waitresses were! They thanked me, walked us to the door, and told us to be careful, since it was still snowing so hard you could barely see. Once we got to the other side of Chugwater, however, and close to Douglas, the storm suddenly lifted and we made it up to Worland without any trouble.

"When we got there, we told my wife, Sharon, and her parents about the nice restaurant we'd found, and so we decided to stop there again on our way back to Denver.

"When Sharon made the return trip with us, the weather was clear and we had no trouble getting to Chugwater," Bob continued. "This was before the highways were fixed, and you had to drive right through the middle of the town. I remembered that as we had come down the hill from Denver heading north, the restaurant had been the third or fourth business on the lefthand side of the street.

"But this time it just wasn't there!" he insisted, sounding as bewildered thirty years later as he must have felt at the time. "There wasn't even any building on the site—we were looking at a vacant lot!"

Unable to believe their eyes, Bob and John walked to a nearby hamburger stand, where Bob spoke to an elderly gentleman.

"I think his name was Charlie, and I told him that we had come through Chugwater and eaten at a restaurant that was no longer there.

" 'Pardon me?' he asked. 'Are you sure this was where you were?'

"And I said, 'I'm positive. That's right where I parked.'

" 'When was this?' Charlie asked, with a funny look on his face.

" 'Eight to ten days ago,' I told him. And then he dropped the bombshell.

" 'Son, the place that you describe burned down years and years ago, and this has been a vacant lot since then.'

" 'There's no way!' I said. 'We were just in there!' And I began to describe both of the waitresses who had served us.

" 'Son,' the man said again, 'that place burned down, and the two people you describe perished in the fire. But that was years and years ago.'

"I looked at John, who had turned a little pale, and he said, 'The best thing we can do is get the hell to Denver!' "

Back in the car, Sharon made light of the situation, believing that the other three were playing a joke on her.

"It was only when Dee became quite anguished and insisted that they were all telling the truth that I believed them," said Sharon. "And after all these years, their story has never changed."

Bob is the first to admit that if he had been alone at the time of the experience, he never would have told anyone about it and would have had serious doubts about his sanity. In fact, all the way back to Denver, the participants in this strange adventure racked their brains for a logical explanation.

"We thought maybe we had never been in Chugwater at all, that maybe we had been in another town," Bob said. "But, hell, there *is* no other town around there. Because on that road you went from Cheyenne to Chugwater to Wheatland to Douglas to Casper to Worland; and we knew that road very well because we traveled it often. And anyway, everything else in the town seemed the same, except that the restaurant was gone."

Looking back on the experience, Bob could recall nothing unusual about the restaurant itself, except for the low cost of the meal. The food and drink, he assured me, seemed real in every way and were much more filling than a mere "ghost" of a dinner would have been. But Bob did remember thinking at the time that the complexions of both waitresses were very white, and later he realized that their long dresses and aprons might have belonged to an earlier time.

How can what happened to Bob and the Greeleys be explained? Bob insists that he doesn't believe in ghosts, but he has no other explanation for what occurred. Could the snowstorm have confused the three travelers so that they didn't know where they were? That seems unlikely, since they were well acquainted with the route, and since there were no other towns along that particular stretch of road from Cheyenne to Douglas. Could atmospheric or other unknown conditions of that blustery day in March 1959 somehow have triggered a flashback into the past?

As bizarre as that theory sounds, it may be the most likely explanation, especially when one considers that other, similar stories have been reported to parapsychologists. The most famous involves two female Oxford dons who, while visiting Versailles on August 10, 1901, were apparently transported for a short while to the Versailles of an earlier time.

Another such trip into the past was reported in an episode of *Arthur C. Clarke's World of Strange Powers*. In this case, two British couples stayed overnight and had dinner at a French inn that they were unable to locate later. The story is very similar to Bob's, in that some of the inn's other customers were wearing old-fashioned clothes, and the bills for both hotel and restaurant were astonishingly inexpensive.

I corresponded with J. Finley Hurley, the author of an upcoming book on inanimate apparitions and "time slips" such as Bob and his friends may have experienced. When I presented the facts of the Chugwater story to him, this was his response:

> It would seem that Bob and his companions either blundered into the past or into an alternate present where the restaurant continued to operate and fashions didn't change—or they were served by apparitions. Concerning the latter explanation, however, there is nothing in the literature of apparitions (including hauntings and such) that could begin to account for the experience. So I must assume the trio wandered into the past. The "very white" complexions of the waitresses (a sour note, that) could simply reflect a time not so long ago when women avoided suntans. In any event, apparitions of the dead aren't the deadly white so popular in folklore. Also, assuming ghosts don't charge for their services, the prices would have been appropriate over a considerable span of time, perhaps into the '50s. I think it's possible that they did have the experience reported.

My next step was to try to check out the facts of Bob's story against the early history of Chugwater. Official records before the town's incorporation in 1919 are practically nonexistent, but oldtimer Russell L. Staats checked his diary and discovered that on March 25, 1959, Chugwater did, indeed, get nine inches of snow. He also believed that a restaurant had existed at one time in the area Bob described.

Chugwater residents Tim and Peggy Dreas did some further scouting around for me, and found another oldtimer who said that almost every business, including a restaurant in the locale described by Bob, had burned to the ground in the first part of the century. No one remembered anyone dying in the blaze, however, but someone did remember a man who roamed around town much like the "Charlie" in Bob's account.

Peggy Dreas told me more about this man. "His name wasn't Charlie, but something similar, such as Ollie, perhaps—so it would have been easy to remember it over the years as Charlie. This fellow apparently had no family and spent most of his time downtown walking the street, so it's very possible that Bob could have spoken to him."

There is another interesting footnote to Bob Wetzel's story. Loren Coleman, in his book *Mysterious America*, lists names of people and places that for unknown reasons are involved more often than others in supernatural occurrences (Boston: Faber and Faber, 1983, 241). Bob's surname is included in that list, and when I informed him of this fact, he laughed and vowed, "Then I'm going to change it to Smith!"

THE SAD SAGA
OF
PRAIRIE ROSE

W hen December winds bluster and howl across the Green Mountains of south central Wyoming, they sometimes bring more than blizzards and bone-chilling cold— several sheep herders, cowboys, and trappers have heard in the moaning gales the plaintive cries of a woman calling, "Help! Help! Oh, God, please help me!"

Ann Robbins was born to a Wyoming ranching couple in the mid-1870s, and from earliest childhood it was clear that she was something special. The strawberry-blonde tomboy's major ambition was to be a cowgirl, and while she was still a teenager, she learned to break her own horses and those of the local ranchers.

When she was old enough to leave home, she joined the C.B. Irwin Wild West Show to ride relay races with Irwin's daughters, but in just a short time, she became one of the top lady bronc riders in the country. She traveled with the troupe for several years before she met and married a cowboy named Henderson, who gave her the stage name that she was to use for the rest of her professional life.

The rodeo circuit meant everything to "Prairie Rose Henderson," whose daring stunts of horsemanship, combined with her exuberance and winning smile, never failed to make her an instant crowd-pleaser. One of her biggest fans was Queen Mary of England, who enjoyed Prairie Rose's act during a command performance of the Tex Austin Rodeo in 1924.

All was not so happy in her personal life, however. Her husband either died or they were divorced, and her next marriage was to Johnny Judd, a great trick roper. Prairie Rose continued to accumulate trophies and prizes for her riding, and in 1917, the Union Pacific Railroad presented her with a gold and silver belt buckle for winning the Ladies' Bronc Riding Championship in Cheyenne.

The late 1920s were the heyday of silent movies, and Johnny Judd and Prairie Rose Henderson moved to Tucson, Arizona, to make westerns. But Prairie Rose tired of that life after a few years, so she returned to Wyoming to make her home, still competing in every major rodeo in the world, including those in Boston and in New York's Madison Square Garden, where she won in her events.

Her third and final husband was a rancher named Charles Coleman, whom she met around 1929. The couple homesteaded in a cabin on Green Mountain, some fifty miles northwest of Rawlins, and little more is known about them until the unusually severe winter of 1932.

One treacherously cold December day when Charles had gone to Rawlins, fifty-seven-year-old Prairie Rose ventured outdoors into a blizzard, probably to check on the animals. She never returned.

Callers at the homestead were the first to discover that something was wrong, when they found the Colemans' dogs locked up in the shed as if their mistress had intended to come back soon. An immediate search of the vicinity was organized, and although the would-be rescuers covered much of the Green Mountains, they were unable to find even a single clue to the former rodeo champion's disappearance.

Not until six and a half years later, in the summer of 1939, was the mystery solved. According to a story dated July 25 in the *Rawlins Republican-Bulletin*, a sheep herder named A. Martinez stumbled upon a skeleton in a comparatively open area of Green Mountain, about one hundred fifty feet from a road. The body was discovered "at the foot of a pine tree in a section partially grown over by sagebrush, in the southern part of Fremont County." All that remained were a few strands of strawberry-blonde hair, some tattered rags that still clung to the bones, and a portion of knotted rope.

Charles Coleman identified the overalls and overshoes found on the body as his wife's, and Coroner M.E. Pickett and Undersheriff Frank Lemoine quickly deduced that she had lost her way and frozen to death in the blizzard, since there was no evidence and very little possibility of foul play. The length of rope found near the body was tied in a square knot, and Charles Coleman identified it as one that he had made for the purpose of catching horses to saddle and ride. According to a July 26 story in the *Rawlins Republican-Bulletin*, Coleman theorized that Prairie Rose had gone out to rope a horse and then became disoriented by the blinding snow. Evidence that he was correct is borne out by the fact that although she was familiar with the area, she had wandered to the opposite side of the mountain, two and a half miles from her own cabin.

An ironic footnote to Prairie Rose's story is that on the day her skeleton was found, her husband was among a crew of firefighters putting out a small blaze only a quarter of a mile from where she lay. The *Republican-Bulletin* also points out the "peculiar twist of fate" in the fact that the body was found in the one small area threatened by the fire, instead of in the "thousands and thousands" of acres where she could have been lost. And the fire, if it had not been controlled, would surely have "erased all trace of the missing woman."

According to western writer and former rodeo performer Don Bell, quite a few people have heard Prairie Rose calling for help on stormy nights. "I didn't know whether what they were telling me was fact or fiction," Don explained, "but I've heard two or three cowboys and sheep herders tell me about the time they heard Prairie Rose's lonesome wailing during blizzards. The last report I heard was as late as the 1960s. Her echo probably still haunts the mountains."

Fiery-spirited, independent Prairie Rose Henderson was a woman way ahead of her time. She could rope and ride far better than most men, and her skill at subduing bucking broncs was legendary. It would seem that the only physical challenge she ever failed to meet was the one that took her life.

LUTHER, THE
(MOSTLY)
LOVABLE HOMEBODY

C arol and Cynthia Barnes obviously like the Victorian era. They named their four daughters after the characters in Louisa May Alcott's *Little Women*, and they live in a beautifully restored nineteenth-century house in Laramie. And even though Meg, Jo, Beth, and Amy, as well as their brother Alexei (named for a character in *The Brothers Karamazov*), have all grown up and moved away, things are still pretty lively at the Barnes residence, thanks to the antics of a charming spirit called Luther, who is himself straight out of the last century.

When the Barneses bought the old stone house in the summer of 1983, they knew nothing about the ghost. It was not until after Carol and Cynthia had signed the final papers that their realtors had second thoughts and showed them a *Laramie Boomerang* article written by Gladys Beery, titled "The Friendly Ghost at 808 Park Street."

"We read the article, and the realtors assured us that they would let us out of the contract if we were at all superstitious," Cynthia said. "But I said that I wasn't afraid of something like that, and that it was all a bunch of baloney. Very frankly, what was worrying me more was the dilapidated condition of the house, and the amount of work it would take to restore it. I jokingly said that when I had first seen the place, I had left a rut up the front sidewalk from dragging my feet, yelling 'No way!' "

The house would take five years to restore completely, and three months of work were necessary before the Barneses could even move in. It was during this time that Carol had his first encounter with the phantom.

"I was working for the food service at the University of Wyoming, and as it was a slow period between the dinner hours on a Sunday afternoon, I came to the house to clean the floor upstairs where I had been plastering. I got rags and soap and water and headed up the stairs. The stairway is built in a curve, and as I rounded one corner, I saw a man in a military uniform standing at the top of the stairs. It startled me so much that I stepped backwards, hit the narrow end of the curved stairway, and fell to the bottom, dislocating eight vertebrae!

"When I finally collected my wits enough to go back upstairs, I found no one, but I thought that maybe there was another way out that I didn't know about. I went to check, but the only way to exit from that level was to jump from one of the windows, and at that time, all of them were sealed shut.

"It was then that I realized I had seen a ghost," Carol said. "I've never seen him clearly since then, and I think it might be because my first reaction was so severe that he didn't want to scare me half to death again! But he seemed completely solid, just like a real person standing there. That's what startled me so much, the thought that I was walking into somebody. I've had these kinds of strange things happen to me all my life, and if I had been able to see through him, I wouldn't have been so shocked!

"He was tall and slender, with dark hair and dark eyes, and a very tailored kind of beard. He looked to be in his middle twenties, maybe thirty at the most. I was within five feet of him, and he was looking at me as if he knew who I was, and was about to say something when I fell.

"He wore a military uniform, but there was no yellow stripe on the pants to indicate that he was in the cavalry. I noticed that he was wearing shoulder epaulets, the mark of an officer; but what struck me as strange was that he had his hat on, and no officer would wear his hat inside a building. I don't know much about uniforms of that period, but he was dressed in blue and was probably in the army of the early frontier."

There is good reason to believe that the soldier was stationed at old Fort Sanders, since the land the house occupies once belonged to the post. Carol Barnes pointed out that because the fort didn't have a special cemetery and usually buried its dead where they fell, the man's bones might be resting underneath the house, especially since there is no basement. There is also speculation that the spirit haunting the Barneses' home may be that of a man killed during a skirmish with Indians, but very little is known for certain.

More is known about the history of the house itself. Several years after Fort Sanders had been abandoned, the land was sold to the city of Laramie and lots were offered for sale. Thomas Birnie, a stonemason from England, bought the property and built the house in 1887 from the same stone used for the territorial prison, which he also helped to construct. The house is made of quarried stone on two sides and fieldstone on the other two.

A worker's wage at that time was forty cents an hour, or about six dollars a day. Even though Birnie worked from daylight to dark, he and his wife Eliza nevertheless lost the house a few years later, because, according to Cynthia Barnes, they had taken out a mortgage with two shyster lawyers and were unable to make the land payments.

The sad early history of the house is, however, not evident from the supernatural phenomena that occur there. The spirit that the Barneses have christened Luther is from all accounts a lighthearted, often mischievous soul who nevertheless watches over his adopted family with concern. Cynthia discovered this side to Luther's personality shortly after moving in.

"Since Carol was working late in those days, coworkers would usually bring me home at about a quarter to six, when it was already dark in the winter," she said. "One night one of them said, 'I thought you told me your husband wasn't here.' When I repeated that he wasn't, she said, 'Well, there's a man standing in your bedroom window upstairs.' I began noticing the same thing myself after another coworker said the same thing. Whenever the house was totally dark and there was no one at home to greet me, there would be the figure of a tall, bearded man standing at that window. It was just as if he were watching to make sure I got home."

"And there's no way that it could be a real person standing up there," Carol interjected, "because he appears between the window and the shade; and even though the sills here are about a foot wide, a real person would be plastered right up against the glass."

Cynthia encountered Luther another time when she was alone in the house. "We had torn the kitchen apart and had put up a stark white wallboard that had not been refinished. I was preparing dinner when something caught my attention. I turned around to see a man's shadow pacing back and forth in front of the wallboard. I couldn't hear any footsteps, but the shadow paced back and forth over about a twelve-foot area. This probably went on for a good five minutes, and I just stopped what I was doing to stand there and watch, trying to convince myself that I wasn't hallucinating. I wasn't frightened, only startled, and I finally decided to get back to fixing supper. I turned around and went back to work, and when I looked around again, the shadow was gone."

According to Cynthia, Luther was to perform even more startling feats. "We had lived in the house for about a year when one night I went to open the kitchen door to let the cat out. One of the steak knives suddenly rose from its slotted wooden holder, floated up into my face, and then fell at my feet! It didn't come toward me in a threatening way, and it wasn't pointed at me, although it was only about six inches from my face. I let out a scream, and my husband came running from the next room. I was really shook up about that!"

Cynthia was equally shaken at another of Luther's little tricks. "One night I had fixed liver for dinner, because I really like it, even though my husband and son don't. They sort of choked some down, leaving a couple pieces on the plate. On the table was also a pitcher of honey to go with the biscuits I had made. Just as I was about to get up to clear away the dishes, this one big piece of liver rose from the plate, floated across the table about eighteen inches, and dropped into the pitcher of honey!

"Carol had gone into the living room to watch TV, but I made him come back to look at the liver in the honey pitcher. He asked, 'What are you doing?' and I explained that I wasn't doing anything, that the liver had levitated off the plate and into the honey by itself. I guess Luther was telling me not to serve that again, since none of the others like it!"

Luther made an even bigger mess another time, when he moved a flour canister four or five feet before tipping it over and dumping its contents all over the room. "Our son and oldest daughter were here with me one evening, and we were all in the living room when we heard this horrible thump in the kitchen," Cynthia recalled. "At first, we blamed the cats, until we realized that they had been with us when we heard the noise. Alexei was about sixteen at the time, and this was his first experience of something that he couldn't rationalize, so he really freaked out!"

The Barneses were never sure why Luther felt compelled to scatter flour all over their kitchen, but they thought they did understand what caused him to go on a rampage another time. "Cynthia and I were getting ready to go to Sheridan for three or four days, and our oldest daughter, Meg, had been sitting in the kitchen doing some sewing," Carol said. "Suddenly, right before her eyes, some inch-and-a-half-long straight pins and quilting pins went flying out of a pincushion and all over the room! Meg screamed, and Cynthia and I ran in to see these pins whirling about everywhere."

"That was apparently Luther's way of letting us know that he doesn't like us to be gone," explained Cynthia, "because when we got back home a few days later, we found Meg sitting on the couch, looking kind of bug-eyed, and she warned us never to leave her alone in the house again. She told us that from the time we had pulled out of the driveway, dresser drawers upstairs had been opening and shutting by themselves, doors started slamming, and jars of canned goods kept banging against each other, sounding as if they were being thrown off the shelves. When she finally got the nerve to investigate, she found all the drawers closed, the doors open, and the jars sitting neatly upright on the shelves. But it wouldn't be long before all the racket started up again, and it didn't stop until the moment we pulled back into the driveway. I guess Luther thinks we're his caretakers, so we're supposed to stay home!"

"He has another endearing habit of moving things around," Cynthia continued. "I once received a set of four little plaques, and because I didn't like them very much, I left them in their boxes and put them in my top bureau drawer, intending to give them away. Well, our bowling team was having a Christmas party, and we each had to present someone with a small gift. I went to get the plaques to wrap them, but they were nowhere to be found. I remembered right where I had put them, and I took everything out of the drawer to look for them, but they weren't there. But wouldn't you know it? They reappeared in that same drawer after the first of January! I guess Luther meant for us to keep them."

Luther was known to move things around even before the Barneses occupied the house. When some college students were renting the place, one of the ghost's favorite pranks was moving a huge potted plant from the parlor to an upstairs bedroom. The residents, who called the spook Garth, often needed help to move the plant back where it belonged.

The Barneses admit that their spirit isn't quite as frolicsome now that all the restoration is finished, but he's still not above rolling up the window shades, one after the other, with a sudden bang to frighten company, and Carol will never forget the time Luther "communicated" with him by means of a chandelier.

"It had five lights on it, and one day I saw one of them go off," he said. "I thought the bulb had burned out, but pretty soon it came back on, so I decided that it wasn't screwed in tightly enough. I didn't bother to fix it, though, and shortly afterwards, another light went off. I began to suspect that Luther was involved, so I asked him to turn one on, then off, then another one on and off, and so on for about thirty minutes, until my daughter Josephine became so unnerved that she asked me to quit. So I said, 'Luther, cut it out!' And all the lights came back on and stayed on."

Luther wasn't quite so cooperative the winter he decided to limit the time that family members could spend in the bathtub. "That was when all the kids except Amy were temporarily staying with us, so there were a lot of people and a lot of confusion," Cynthia recalled. "We have a large bathroom, with a small light by the mirror and a larger one in the ceiling. Whenever anyone would get into the bathtub, he would have exactly five minutes before the light went off! Carol changed lightbulbs about five times, and he checked the wiring in the switch, but there was no short. And it wasn't just that the light would go off; the switch would actually flip off! And if you tried to flip the switch again, the light wouldn't come back on.

"It was frustrating, especially for me, since I like to get in the tub and read. And with that many people in the house, it was the only time I had to myself. But do you know, as soon as the kids started leaving again, we never had any more trouble with that light."

While Luther's ways are sometimes maddening, they are more often well-meaning and helpful. Long before the Barneses moved in, the ghost had a reputation for emptying and cleaning ashtrays, a favor he performed for previous residents Steve and Marsha Oakes, as well as for the college students mentioned previously. Right after Carol and Cynthia bought the house, they rented out an apartment in the back and soon discovered that Luther was providing the same service for these tenants.

"The way the house was divided, my breaker box was in their apartment," Carol explained. "And since I was doing some rewiring in the house, I often had to go there when they were gone to turn the breakers on and off. One day, the young lady happened to come home from school as I was leaving, and she said she was so very sorry that their ashtrays bothered me, and that if they'd known I was going to come in, they would have emptied them before they went to school. I asked her what in the world she was talking about, and she said, 'Every time you come over, we notice that all our ashtrays are emptied and cleaned.' I told her that I certainly wasn't doing it, since I don't even clean my own ashtrays very well!"

Luther also undoubtedly believed he was helping out when he showed his disapproval of some wallpaper Carol had bought for Alexei's room. "Because there was practically none to be found at any of the stores at that time, I had bought a design that I didn't particularly care for," he said. "And just when I had gotten one wall completed, some students from the university came by to see how the renovation was progressing. We were downstairs for half an hour, and when all three of us later tramped upstairs and went into my son's bedroom, I gasped and everybody stopped abruptly. All of the paper that I had put up, about seven or eight strips that had gone from ceiling to floor, had been very neatly taken off the wall and laid face down across the floor. I knew that Luther had done it, because when wallpaper falls off by itself, it doesn't fall neatly; it just slides down the wall.

"Since that episode, we've discovered that whenever Luther doesn't like something we're doing, he lets us know. But on the positive side, he's apparently helped us to find unusual things to redo the house. If I want a particular thing, I'll think about it for several days; then suddenly I'll get this overwhelming urge to go somewhere, and the article I want will be there, at a ridiculously low price.

"When I was doing the library in tones of brown and pink, for example, I decided that I wanted an Oriental rug with a chocolate background and pink roses. I had never seen one in my entire life, but I wanted it simply because it would fit in there. One afternoon I got an urge to go to a pawnshop that I had never been to before. And sure enough, here was this rug, exactly as I had envisioned it, and exactly the right size for the room, which is of a very odd size.

"So now I've learned to rely upon these urges, which may be a form of telepathy," Carol explained. "No matter what I want, I just set it in my mind; then I'll forget about it until I get the urge to go someplace. And when I do, I generally find whatever I'm looking for. Other people have even started to rely on me to find things for them, too, and I can usually get them at a good price."

The Barnes family has also learned to rely upon Luther to warn them when it is necessary to exercise caution in both their personal and professional lives. "We often get a lot of activity if something is about to happen to us, and we've learned to be very careful at those times with relationships, business dealings, employment, whatever. We start looking for problems, and generally we have good cause to do so."

Luther's input was crucial in Carol's decision to leave his job at the university, for example. "The work itself was getting me down, the stress was extremely high, and I was even having chest pains the last year I was there. I had been toying with the idea of resigning, but I was just staying out of sheer stubbornness. At that time we started hearing what sounded like a car running into the walls, and in a stone house, that's quite a noise, and the whole structure would vibrate! The first night, I was the only one who heard it, while everyone else kept right on sleeping. This went on from about midnight until four in the morning, and after it had gone on for several days, I finally realized I was being warned. I said, 'All right, I'll quit the university,' and the noise stopped."

Both Carol and Cynthia admit that they never feel alone in the house, that they sense someone is protecting them, and that they have often found themselves talking to an unseen presence. Both the Barnes and the Oakes families mentioned seeing a hazy shape at the foot of their beds from time to time, but no one has ever been frightened. "It's as if you wake up to see a friend standing there, so you go right back to sleep," Carol explained.

Luther's loving concern extends not only to the adults he lives with, but to children and pets as well. The five Oakes children who lived in the house were all thrilled to have their "own" ghost, and the dogs of both families often seemed to be playing with an unseen someone. "When we moved in here," Cynthia said, "we had a pit bull, golden lab cross, and a teacup-sized Boston bull terrier. And those two dogs would go upstairs and romp like they were playing with somebody, not with each other. And Marsha and Steve Oakes said that their dog was always very aware of something in the house that they weren't able to see.

"Luther has also checked up on our grandson from time to time. When Meg and her family were staying in the little rental house that sits on our lot, her husband, Tony, used to chuckle about our experiences with the ghost. But one night he told us that he was convinced that Luther really exists. For several nights he had heard footsteps going down the hall to his son Seth's room. He had never heard them leave, and when he went to check, he found nobody there. So he decided that Luther wasn't just someone we had invented to amuse ourselves."

Further experiences involving their grandchildren made Carol and Cynthia wonder if perhaps other entities besides Luther were also residing on their property. "One night about eleven o'clock we heard this little child talking to us, and we thought that Seth had gotten away from the little house and had come over here," Carol recalled. "I kept telling him to come into the living room, but he never did. Seth was about two then, and we kept hearing the kind of gibberish you'd expect from a child of that age, so Cynthia and I got up and started to look for him. We never found anyone, and when we checked at our daughter's place, Seth was sound asleep in his bed. Even after we came back home, however, until about one or two o'clock in the morning, we kept hearing this child talking in different areas of the house. This has happened several times over the past two years, but we've never been able to dig through the archives to find out whether any children have died here.

"It's interesting, though, because Seth and the other grandkids sometimes talk about playing upstairs with someone they call Joshua," Carol continued, "but we assume from the things they say that Joshua is not a child, but an adult. But their use of the name 'Joshua' has always puzzled us, because it's not the name of anyone we know, and even though it's become popular again in the last few years, it doesn't seem like a name they would make up."

Strange things continue to happen at the Barnes residence, and Cynthia, who once doubted the existence of the supernatural, is now a believer. "Having Luther around has been quite an experience," she admitted. "Until I lived in this house, I always snickered at people who told stories about spirits, and I thought they were nuts. But now I've found out that they really weren't. I'm firmly convinced!"

CURSE
OF THE
INDIAN SKULL

D o spirits of the dead really return to haunt the living when their remains are disturbed? Many ghost stories, including several in this book, are premised upon just this theory. While there are those who consider such an idea to be superstitious nonsense, they should at least consider the story of the Eloxite Company before making up their minds.

Located in Wheatland, in the southeast corner of the state, the Eloxite Company is a wholesale jewelry findings establishment, selling everything the artist or hobbyist needs to fashion such items as bracelets, rings, or bola ties. Formerly, in the front half of the building, the company housed a small museum specializing in rock specimens and Indian artifacts.

In the mid to late '70s, the museum acquired an Indian skull from a Lincoln, Nebraska, trader who had unearthed it from the hills of western Iowa. Little was known about the individual to whom it had belonged, except that he or she had probably been a member of one of the tribes of the Woodland Indians who previously inhabited parts of the Midwest.

The skull was put on display for quite some time, until the company ran out of room and decided to dispose of the museum. Employees packed up the display items, boxed them, and stored them in various places. The skull was put into a box in the storeroom in the basement.

According to employee Bob Berry, that's when strange things began to happen. "One evening we were working downstairs, and we heard a big crash," he said. "We went into the storeroom, and the box with the skull in it was on the floor. The skull wasn't damaged, but four or five other boxes filled with odds and ends like pots, pans, and display racks were dumped out onto the floor." Puzzling over the cause of the commotion, the employees replaced everything in the boxes and put them back up on the shelf where they belonged.

According to Bob Berry, it was not long afterwards that more eerie events began to occur. "For one thing," he said, "we had some suitcases stacked in the back hallway at the top of a flight of stairs. My apartment was adjoining the hallway. In the middle of the night, for no good reason, they all fell down the stairs!" Bob also pointed out that no intruders could have broken in and caused the racket, because both doors, at the top and bottom of the stairs, were locked.

"We also had an expensive French oil painting hanging upstairs. And again, for no good reason, in the middle of the day, it fell off the wall and onto a coffee mug, was pierced in the center, and we had to have it repaired," Bob said. "And another large print, hanging on a wall in vice president Greg Ackerman's apartment downstairs, came crashing down about two o'clock one morning."

Bob added that by this time, things were falling down all the time, both day and night. "Our apartments were in the bottom of the building, and the offices were in the top, and in the middle of the night, we often heard something fall upstairs. Then we would go up there and find different kinds of things on the floor, including merchandise off the shelves."

Another time Bob and a local doctor were walking across the hallway in the downstairs part of the building when a crowbar suddenly jumped from a shelf onto the cement floor and bounced a couple of times.

"Doc said, 'Who threw that?' And I said, 'I don't know!'" Bob remembered. "And then we went over and picked it up and put it back where it had been.

"We began to get pretty tired of things falling down all the time, and we got to thinking that maybe it had something to do with that Indian skull. So we called up a mortuary in Council Bluffs, Iowa, and they said for us to ship it to them UPS. They then reburied it for us in an Indian burial ground near Council Bluffs. This happened, I believe, in 1984, and we haven't had any trouble like that since."

Was the Indian skull responsible for the poltergeist activity at the Eloxite Company in Wheatland? And if so, why did no odd events occur until *after* the skull had been removed from the museum? Can we infer from this fact that the spirit of its former owner did not mind the skull's being on public display, but did strenuously object to its being boxed away and forgotten? While the answers to these questions are not readily answerable, the employees of the Eloxite Company are at least satisfied that they have removed the cause of their haunting.

KNOCK
THREE
TIMES

L oud, unexplained crashes, rattles, and bangs—the proverbial Things that Go Bump in the Night—are among the most common manifestations of the poltergeist. And while these so-called "noisy ghosts" are often associated with adolescents, it isn't unknown for an older person to become the focus of such activity as well. Could that be what happened to Bob Lynn?

In the summer of 1977 when he was twenty-four, Bob moved into a small house on the south side of Powell, in northwest Wyoming. "One night when I had some friends over," he remembered, "we were playing the stereo so loud that we had to raise our voices to be heard. Suddenly we heard a loud bang-bang-bang coming from the wall, the blows so hard that a plaque on an opposite wall almost fell from its hook. I jumped up to look out the door, but no one was there.

"We lowered the volume on the stereo, and I positioned myself so that I could see anybody who walked into the front yard. After about forty-five minutes, we heard the pounding again. The sounds were obviously coming from the outside wall, so I must have been looking right through whoever was hitting it!

"Shortly after this, two girls arrived who had just been to see, of all things, *The Exorcist.* Thanks to the movie, they were nervous, anyway, and one of them left as soon as we told her what had happened. The other girl stayed about an hour, and while we were talking, we heard the loud knocks for the third time!"

Bob's former girlfriend, Carmen Consalvo, pointed out that this same pattern of threes figured in many of the strange happenings at the house. Not long after the wall-knocking episode, for example, Bob was in bed but not asleep one night when he heard three loud hits apparently coming from the floor under his bed.

"Another time, when we came back from a trip, we discovered that the pipes had frozen, and Bob had to go underneath the house to thaw them out," said Carmen. "Before he went down, he told me to turn on the hot water tank as soon as I heard him knock three times on the floor under the bathroom.

"He had to crawl to get where he needed to be, so I figured it would take him a few minutes. But almost immediately, I heard the three knocks under the bathroom floor. I turned on the hot water, and the next thing I knew, Bob came through the front door. He hadn't even gone under the house yet!"

The eeriest experience of all occurred when Bob was alone one day. "I had been wearing headphones and playing with my tape recorder and guitar," he said. "I shut off the recorder for a few seconds to stretch out and relax. Everything was completely silent except for a little bit of background hiss from the recording equipment, when suddenly it sounded as if a catastrophe were taking place in the kitchen.

"I thought surely that someone had broken in and was demolishing the entire room—smashing dishes, crashing the chair legs into the table, ripping hinges loose and yanking nails out of wood. I heard my plastic plates smacking against each other and bouncing off the wall, and glasses sounded as if they were shattering all over the floor. Yet there weren't any human noises, just the sounds of the objects themselves being propelled through the air.

"The commotion continued for about forty-five seconds. At first I was stunned and afraid to move, but finally I got my nerve up and cautiously peeked around the wall into the kitchen. As I stood there looking in, the sounds of random destruction persisted for another eight or ten seconds—but absolutely nothing was out of place! Not one thing had been disturbed in the entire room. And then, as abruptly as it started, the noise just quit—as if someone had recorded it and then switched off the tape. I had some real nervous shivers after that experience!"

Hearing the sounds of a room being destroyed, when in fact everything in it remains quite motionless, is very common in poltergeist cases. What is perhaps not so common is the noise Bob heard one afternoon while he was on the telephone.

"I was talking to Chris, the girl who had been at my house the night we heard the pounding on the wall," he explained. "I was sitting in an unused bedroom just across the hall from the bathroom when I heard a hissing, crackling sound, the kind you would make if you wadded up a newspaper and rolled it around. It was faint at first; then it grew louder, and Chris said she could hear it over the phone. In fact, she said that it blended with my voice so that I was hard to understand. As I listened more carefully, I noticed that the sound was coming from the bathroom. There was no electronic equipment there, but it sounded something like tape hiss, only more crackly.

"I told Chris that I was going to investigate, and as I walked into the bathroom, at first I went right past the sound. Then I went through it and in front of it, and when I located exactly where it was, I carefully moved toward it. It was about a foot and a half above the floor, so I sank onto my hands and knees and moved my head so that the sound was all around it. It was just a ball of sound, approximately eighteen inches in diameter. The sound persisted for about a minute; then it stopped as abruptly as the chaos in the kitchen had done."

Bob has no explanation for the strange ball of sound, but similarly bizarre noises have been recorded in other poltergeist cases. Not all manifestations of poltergeists are aural, however. Some are visual, and occasionally, as at Bob's house, even apparitions may be seen.

For example, nearly everyone who spent any length of time in the living room reported catching a glimpse of someone passing quickly by a window, apparently heading toward the front door. And yet, when the door was opened, no one was there.

"This happened so many times," Bob said, "that eventually I didn't bother getting up unless I heard somebody knocking. Only once, on a warm day in 1979, did I catch more than the blurred image of somebody going past. I was looking out the east window when I saw a young Mexican girl walk by. She appeared to be between fifteen and eighteen years old, with shiny black hair that came almost to her knees. She was wearing blue jeans, a fringed leather vest, and a short-sleeved shirt. She had a very nice shape, but I couldn't see her face, because it was turned away and hidden by her hair.

"Six or eight seconds passed before I decided to go out the door to get a better look. But when I went outside, there was no sign of anybody else in the entire neighborhood! There were no trees or bushes large enough for anyone to hide behind, and my house was not close enough to any others that she could have popped into one of them," Bob continued. "So if a young girl really was there, she must have just *flown* to get out of sight so quickly. I still wonder if she was made of flesh and blood!"

Bob apparently witnessed another apparition on a dark, clear night when there was no moon. "I saw what appeared to be a fairly large man standing near the mailbox on the southeast corner of the property," he said. "He was facing away from me, so at first I saw his silhouette. Then he turned, looked at me, and disappeared in the blink of an eye. At the same time, a tree near the mailbox began to give off a strange glow."

After this sighting, Bob and Carmen began referring to their ghost as George, and they blamed him whenever anything odd happened. But the history of the house might provide a clue to the man's real identity. Before Bob lived there, it was the residence of a man who drowned in a boating accident on the Buffalo Bill Reservoir. Could he be the one responsible for the various strange occurrences in the house?

According to well-known parapsychologist William G. Roll, poltergeist phenomena "are usually associated with a living person; in fact, it seems to have become part of the meaning of poltergeist that there be such a connection" ("Poltergeists" in Benjamin D. Wolman, ed., *Handbook of Parapsychology*, New York: Van Nostrand Reinhold Company, 1977, 382-383). Therefore, Roll continues, this suggests that the events may be produced by the person's own psychokinetic energy, or perhaps by "an incorporeal entity which has attached itself to him or her" (383).

Since the events described in this chapter, Bob's life has changed in many respects, and those changes have influenced the way he now views the whole subject of psychic phenomena. "I have become Christian," he said, "and I believe that the lion's share of paranormal experiences are probably Satanic in origin." He does admit, however, that his own energies may also have played a role in the events that occurred.

"From 1972 to 1976, I was around a lot of people in Colorado who were interested in the paranormal," he explained, "and when I came back to Powell in 1977, I brought with me a studied appreciation for these things. That's when I moved into the house, and things started happening almost immediately."

Bob also believes that his own insecurities at the time might have contributed to the problem, because when things in his life began to run more smoothly, the phenomena disappeared. And while his brother and other people occasionally had strange experiences in the house when Bob wasn't there, Bob wonders whether his own sensitivity might not have passed to them by the power of suggestion.

So what is the real explanation for the uncanny phenomena at the little house on the south side of Powell? No one—at least no one this side of the grave—knows for sure.

THE OLDTIMER'S STORY

F red Cozzens labels himself a skeptic when it comes to matters of the supernatural. But a story told to him by an oldtime cowpoke over thirty years ago still has the power to raise goosebumps on his flesh and make cold chills run down his spine.

"I first heard Bugs Jenkins's* story over thirty years ago, and he was already an old man then. But when he was young, he and another cowboy were working for someone in Kerwin, an old mining town up the Wood River out of Meeteetse. One night, the two of them were caught in a blizzard there and realized that they couldn't make it back to camp. They felt lucky to find an abandoned building to shelter them from the storm, and they tied up their horses where they would be safe and walked into what had obviously been the old saloon.

"The bar was still in place, as were the tables and chairs. Bugs said that the wind was making a terrible racket with all the loose-fitting doors and windows rattling and banging and whistling. The intensity of the storm didn't scare the men, though, since they were relatively safe inside.

"They had been joking and laughing over their predicament, but suddenly they stopped and looked at each other in disbelief. Both of them had heard the unmistakable sounds of voices besides their own, as well as a moaning noise that was definitely not the howling of the wind. The sounds got louder and louder, and although both men were scared to stay inside the old saloon, they were more scared of freezing to death if they went outdoors.

"Finally, they positioned themselves with their backs to the old boiler. The guy with Bugs held his gun cocked and ready across his lap all night, half expecting something to attack him. As you can imagine, neither of them slept a wink. They just sat there and listened to the mysterious sounds all around them. It was just as if the old saloon had come alive again!

"They never heard the voices clearly, although they could make out a few words now and then. Most of the time, it sounded like everybody was in good spirits, although there were occasional sounds of fighting, too. No gunshots or anything, just the angry voices of some old boys arguing. You can imagine that those two cowpokes were real tickled to get out of that saloon the next morning!

"Bugs told me this story when he was herding sheep, and I was a camp tender for him up on the Beartooth Mountains," Fred explained. "I probably heard him tell it two or three times, and I never saw a listener yet who didn't have cold chills as though he was the one sitting by that boiler, expecting any minute to have something come and get him! And I never knew Bugs to be flustered or scared of anything in his life. But whenever he told that story, you could hear the fear in his voice and see the change of expression on his face, because it was just as though he had really gone back to that night."

THE PAST
NEVER DIES AT
FORT LARAMIE

Thereʼs no way to guarantee that anyone will see, hear, or otherwise experience psychic phenomena at any given time or place, but there are locations where the odds of witnessing supernatural occurrences seem to be greater. The Fort Laramie National Historic Site at Fort Laramie, Wyoming, is certainly such a place. It may very well be the most haunted spot in the state, judging from the number of eerie happenings that have been reported there.

No battle was ever fought at the lone outpost on the empty plain, but the rich and varied past of Fort Laramie is nevertheless responsible for a great many phantom sights and sounds over the years. Founded as a fur-trading center in 1834, the post was taken over by the army in the early days of western expansion, with a new mission of protecting travelers on the Oregon Trail from hostile Indians and other dangers.

For the last eight years, a "living history" class has been conducted during the third week of May on the grounds of the old fort. University of Wyoming professor Don Warder coordinates the training program for the course, which attempts to replicate the third week in May 1876.

"There was a lot of hustle and bustle at the post at that time," he explained. "It was just before General Crook took all but twenty-nine of the fort's soldiers to fight his battle on the Rosebud, just before Custer was wiped out on the Little Bighorn."

Those participating in the class learn firsthand what life at the fort was like more than one hundred years ago, not only for the soldiers, but for others, such as laundresses and wives of officers and enlisted men as well.

"Anyone who has spent a lot of time at Fort Laramie knows that you can almost feel the presence of the past as a tangible thing," said Denny Dreher, who has taught the course along with Don Warder. "You *know* what it was like, because the shadows are still there, and the old fort seems to be alive yet, maybe just on another level of existence. The feeling that you've somehow become part of the past is unbelievably strong when you're standing out on the parade ground just as the sun is setting."

This feeling of oneness with the past has been reported by virtually all of the participants in the living history program, and it is often an uncanny sensation, as Don Warder will attest.

"A couple of years ago, a group of about six or eight of us were working to get things ready for the course. We were staying in the same barracks where the soldiers had slept, and the bunks were reproductions of the originals," he said. "We had been working all day, so we were pretty tired when we went to bed. I don't sleep very regularly, and around two o'clock in the morning, another fellow and I heard what sounded like two doors slamming, about five seconds apart.

"My initial thought was that one of the security guards had come in to make sure that the doors were locked and had slammed some of them in the process," he explained. "But the next morning when I talked to the man who had been on duty at the time, he said that he had not even come into the building, since he knew we were there.

"Two really strange things about this experience were that we had locked all the outer doors when we went to bed, and all of the interior doors had been temporarily removed from their hinges during the restoration of the building. So what doors did we hear slamming in the night, and who was slamming them?"

An even more puzzling occurrence took place an hour or so later that same night. "A graduate student sleeping just across the room from me suddenly bolted up from her pillow, screaming and crying," Dr. Warder continued. "She wasn't sure whether she had been dreaming or not, but she had felt something come down the center aisle between the bunks, brush against her feet, then move around to her bedside, where it had breathed hot air onto her neck.

"I was awake before she started to scream, so if an animal had gotten into the barracks, I definitely would have known about it," Dr. Warder insisted. "But regardless of what frightened her, she was so upset that one of the men walked her to the administration building, where the two of them stayed drinking coffee until daybreak."

Dr. Warder added that during those same few days, the group experienced yet another unexplained occurrence. "We were sitting on the porch of a building called Quarters A, listening to a tape of a retreat parade over the loudspeakers. When the tape ended, I looked up toward the post surgeon's house, and I'll swear to this day that I saw a kerosene lantern in the window!

"Now what you have to understand," he pointed out, "is that Fort Laramie is kept totally dark at night on purpose. Lights are against park service policy—for one thing, there is no electricity in most of the buildings, and no one leaves battery driven lights inside any of them, either. Kerosene lamps are not allowed in buildings unless someone is there to watch them, so there was no reason for a light to be on in the surgeon's quarters or anywhere else.

"Naturally, we were all curious, so we got up and walked to the house," Dr. Warder continued, "and as we drew nearer, the light disappeared. Just as soon as I stepped onto the porch, however, the hair on the back of my neck stood up, and I started having goosebumps and cold chills. Denny Dreher had an even stronger reaction—he was so unnerved that he wouldn't set one foot upon the porch!

"I was still shaking when I unlocked the door with my pass key and walked inside," admitted Dr. Warder. "But the minute I did so, the frightening sensation simply disappeared, and I found nothing out of order at all."

Don Warder never used to give much credence to the supernatural, but his experiences at Fort Laramie have made him a believer. "I've come to think that various time periods can exist simultaneously, and this phenomenon might explain some of the strange things that have happened at the fort. About two years ago, for example, we had a lot of rain and late spring snow during the course, and one evening the students were standing guard duty all night long, as the soldiers used to do. Around eleven o'clock, another instructor and I went together to check on them.

"One of the men was in a very isolated position, about a hundred yards down behind the Officers' Row, close to the Laramie River. As we walked toward him with our lantern, a medium rain was falling and a light fog lay on the ground, but it was certainly not enough to obscure visibility. Up until the time we walked right up and spoke to this guard, however, he never saw us, never noticed our light coming toward him.

"That in itself was very unusual, but even more so was the fact that about twenty minutes before we came along, the guard had been walking a twenty-yard straight line when he sensed someone approaching him. He lowered his rifle and put a challenge to this unknown person, as he was supposed to do, but there was no one there. I've talked with the fellow since then, and he still swears to this day that someone walked up to him that night."

Dr. Warder has also heard stories from other people who have spent time at Fort Laramie during the evening hours. "The park sometimes has moonlight tours, when the buildings stay open later than usual," he explained. "Just as in the daytime, interpreters play the roles of people who might have lived in the buildings. One summer, a young woman had been assigned to work in Quarters A, the former home of officers. In the role of a lieutenant's wife, she greeted visitors on the porch and sometimes led them into the main living room, where she asked them to excuse the shabby furnishings, since her husband didn't make much money. As she continued describing the life of a newly married woman at the fort, she would sometimes hear shuffling noises coming from an upstairs bedroom.

"For a long time, the young woman thought the noises had a logical explanation. After all, she was dating a fellow who was also working at the fort as a summer seasonal, and it would have been easy enough for him to sneak in the back door, go up the stairs, and shuffle around in the bedroom to try to scare her. So when she heard these noises, she would step out of character just long enough to let the visitors know that her boyfriend was upstairs playing a trick on her.

"One day, however, she had just explained things to her audience when the boyfriend himself came walking across the parade ground. The young woman fled Quarters A at once and refused to go back. When her boyfriend found out what had happened, he went in to check the building, but there was no one there.

"Several security guards have occasionally noticed a light in the window of that same bedroom, after hours and after dark," Dr. Warder continued. "To get up there when the building is closed requires unlocking both the front door and the door to the room itself, and when they've done all that, they've never found anyone inside. There's also a rocking chair in the room, and I've been told that the guards have seen it still swaying back and forth. After double checking the quarters and securing the doors once more, the men have sometimes gotten only a few steps from the building before seeing a light in the window again! After inspecting everything one more time and having the light reappear, anyway, some of them have finally just shrugged their shoulders and walked away!"

Dr. Warder's adventuring spirit has led him to explore Quarters A and every other building at the fort between the hours of midnight and 3 A.M. "I usually go after all the students have gone to bed. I just want to see whether anything will happen while I'm there," he said. "Apparently a woman died in Quarters A in the 1930s, but although I've sat for an hour or so inside the closet in the bedroom where all these disturbances have occurred, I've never observed anything."

Don Warder's friend and colleague, Denny Dreher, has had his share of spooky happenings at the fort as well. In addition to the time when he was too frightened to step up onto the porch of the surgeon's quarters, he has experienced eerie phenomena in Old Bedlam, the earliest existing military structure in the state of Wyoming.

Built in the 1850s, the building served for a time as the bachelor officers' quarters, where the wild times of the inhabitants soon gave it its nickname. The structure also housed the commanding officers' headquarters for a while, and the upstairs was actually a hotel in the late 1870s and '80s. Different parts of Old Bedlam have been restored to represent the various eras of its history, and Denny Dreher was staying in a vacant room on the west side when the following strange things occurred.

"I spent five nights there in the spring of 1986, sharing the room with another fellow involved in the living history program," he explained. "One time, around three o'clock in the morning, we heard the sounds of furniture scraping around on the floor right below us, in the section of the building that is part of the old bachelor officers' quarters. It sounded just as if people were rearranging the room. We were both so tired that we didn't get up to investigate, but after talking with the security people the next day, we learned that they had not been in the building. In fact, the doors had all been locked, so no one had admittance to Old Bedlam other than my roommate and I. I guess the spirits were restless that evening!

"A few nights later, I had gone back to our room at about a quarter to six to change clothes for the dress retreat parade being held that evening. I was the only one in the building, and the doors and windows were all shut, so there shouldn't have been any breezes blowing through. But as I was changing into my uniform, a trap door in the ceiling right above my head suddenly seemed to be sucked up into the attic, and the space was open!

"It startled me, but I didn't have time to investigate, since I was due out on the parade ground for the ceremony. The next day I told the park service what had happened, and they came to fix the trap door, but they couldn't explain why it had flown open like that.

"One of the most recent stories at Fort Laramie involves a park service employee who had gone out to raise the colors at sunrise," Denny Dreher continued. "Just as he was putting the flag up, the employee thought he heard voices, so he stopped and looked around him, but saw nothing. He resumed raising the colors and heard more voices behind him. This time one of them said, 'It's certainly taking that man a long time to get the flag up!'

"At that, the employee glanced quickly over his shoulder and saw two officers in military blue standing right behind him. But when he whirled around to face them, they had disappeared.

"One of the best-known stories at the fort involves two young women, seasonal employees, who were sitting and talking on the porch of Old Bedlam," Denny Dreher added. "Suddenly they heard a rap on the window behind them, and a face peered out from behind the curtains and commanded, 'Hold it down out there! We're having a meeting in here.' The word is that the women wasted no time getting down from the porch, since it was well known that the building was empty!"

Not all the mysterious occurrences at Fort Laramie involve seeing or hearing strange things. Doug Johnson, who did volunteer work there for at least ten years, experienced an overwhelming feeling of despair emanating from the decaying residence to the west of Old Bedlam. Formerly used for officers' housing, the duplex no longer has a floor or roof, and only the lime grout concrete walls are left standing.

"Basically, I kept having the disturbing sense that something cruel had happened in that house," Doug Johnson said. "At first, I tried to ignore the feeling, but in 1984, I began to envision what might have taken place there. I came to believe that child abuse had occurred over a relatively long period, possibly sexual abuse of a daughter, and the beating of the sons, maybe because the father didn't want them to tell his secret.

"I've never had feelings like that about a place before, and in all the time I've spent at Fort Laramie, I've never experienced any of the ghostly manifestations that others have reported. But every time I looked into a window on the right side of that structure, I had the feeling that that room was where the abuse had occurred."

Doug Johnson talked about his feelings to historian Don Rickey, who has lately done a lot of research on the paranormal. "Don and I have known each other for quite some time, and he told me that because I worked for years with socially and emotionally disturbed children, I might be more attuned to these types of situations," Doug explained.

Interestingly enough, one of the employees at the fort was checking records a few years ago and discovered that a lieutenant had been dishonorably discharged from Fort Laramie for physically abusing his wife. Don Warder pointed out that records in the Victorian era would not have been so explicit as to name incest or sexual abuse of wives or children, so this family tragedy may have been the one sensed by Doug Johnson, even though there was no indication of where the lieutenant had lived.

Of all those who have been employed at Fort Laramie, however, surely no one has had more encounters with the supernatural than former security guard O. A. "Steve" Caligiore. Many of his eerie experiences have taken place in Quarters A, the former officers' duplex that may hold the honor of being the most haunted building at the fort.

One of Steve Caligiore's jobs was to make sure that all the buildings were locked up each night after the tourists had left. Time and again, however, he would secure the locks on the doors to Quarters A, only to find them unbolted when he made his next rounds.

"I would walk in the front door on the east side, being careful to lock the door behind me," he explained. "Then I would walk through the building to the back door and secure it before re-entering Quarters A through the back door on the west side. I would then bolt both the back and front doors of that part of the building, and as often as not, when I came back around to the first door I had locked, it would be wide open and the tumbler would be turned up!"

Each time this happened, Steve Caligiore checked Quarters A for intruders, but none were ever found. When he finally mentioned the trouble he was having to other guards, they often smiled knowingly, and some admitted that the same thing had happened to them.

The doors that wouldn't stay locked were only the beginning of his troubles, however. "As I went through Quarters A to lock up, I had to pass by an antique icebox right in the middle of the hallway," he continued. "For some reason, the lid was often open, and I always put it back on. But whenever I came back through, the darned thing would be off again!"

The security guard began to sense that an unseen presence was responsible for the unexplained occurrences in Quarters A, and one night he received dramatic evidence that this was so.

"On this particular evening, I had just locked the front door and was about to lock the back when I suddenly felt something grab me on the shoulder from behind! It felt just like a human hand, fingers and all, but as I swung my heavy flashlight around to hit whoever it was, I encountered only empty space."

The phantom arm-grabber was to strike again, but its next victims were visitors passing through Quarters A. "It was almost closing time, so I took them through the building and explained its history to them," Steve Caligiore continued, "and since it was late, I locked the doors when we left. When we got outside, I noticed that two young women were giggling, so I asked them what was so funny.

" 'We don't know,' one of them said. 'You were in front of us, so it couldn't have been you, but it seemed like somebody was grabbing our arms the whole time we were in there!'

"Another night, I took four couples through Quarters A, and when we started through the door, one of the ladies turned to her husband and asked, 'What are you doing?' He looked startled and said, 'I'm not doing anything,' but she insisted that someone had tapped her on the shoulder, as if to draw her attention to something in one of the rooms.

"I don't know where I came up with the name George, but every time something happens in that building, I say that George did it. Sometimes I've told him, 'George, I know you're there, so just leave us alone. We would like to go through these buildings without your interfering!' And usually, when I've done that, he's stopped whatever he was doing, although I have had to remind him to keep the doors locked!

"One time when I was working days instead of the graveyard shift, I got a call on the radio to come check out Quarters A. Some park employees were doing inventory of the items in each room, and they had suddenly heard some kind of racket upstairs. I went right down there, and I heard the noise, too, as if an animal were trapped somewhere in the attic. I climbed up and had a good look around with my flashlight, but I didn't find traces of a bird or anything. Once in the attic, I couldn't hear a bit of noise, but I checked the walls and still found nothing.

"As soon as I had reported back to the office, here came another call on the radio to return to Quarters A. I went back and checked again, but still found nothing. After this had happened to me two or three times, a whole crew from maintenance came out to see what they could find. We heard the noise again, and thought that maybe a snake was crawling inside the walls. But when we shone our lights down between the studs, we still didn't find anything to account for the sounds."

Quarters A has had a bad reputation for years. A former curator refused to go into the building, and according to Steve Caligiore, only a few employees at the park have ever been able to stay in it alone. Does the history of Quarters A provide any possible reasons for the haunting?

"Yes, according to gossip around the fort, two or three incidents supposedly occurred there," explained the security guard. "Different versions of the story exist, but one is that a fur trader who lived here used to lock his daughter up to keep her from going out with any of the officers or enlisted men. But whenever he went out of town, she would get out and start flirting with the soldiers. One day she was about to elope, but her father returned and surprised the couple just as they were making their escape. Then he apparently beat his daughter severely."

Could this story possibly have something to do with the child abuse that Doug Johnson sensed in the house next to Old Bedlam? Or is it a variant of the tale of the Lady in Green, the most famous ghost story of Fort Laramie, if not of the entire state of Wyoming?

Much has been written about this beautiful phantom who is said to appear once every seven years, so I will give only a brief summary here. Apparently, no one alive today has seen her, but in 1951, Colonel P.W. Allison of Salem, Oregon, returned to the fort, where he granted an interview concerning his father's sighting of the ghost in 1871.

The young Lieutenant Allison of the Second Cavalry arrived at Fort Laramie fresh from West Point, and he was the proud possessor of a fine thoroughbred horse and a large hunting dog that was half Russian wolfhound. Soon after arriving, he joined a group of young officers on a wolf hunt along the hills east of the fort, and as his horse was superior to those of the other men, he soon left his companions far behind.

Later, as he rode down from the hills to return to the fort, his horse began limping, so he removed a stone from one of her shoes. As he was remounting, he saw a lone rider galloping away eastward. At first, Lieutenant Allison was afraid that he had spotted an Indian waving a signal blanket, but upon closer inspection, he saw that it was a young woman riding sidesaddle, dressed in an old-fashioned green riding habit and a feathered hat.

Allison believed her to be a newly arrived visitor to the fort, and he started toward her in an attempt to warn her of the dangers of riding so far out alone. But before he could get near her, she raised her quirt to whip her fine black horse, and off the animal dashed, out of sight over a rise of ground.

The young lieutenant gave chase, but was dumbfounded upon reaching the crest of the hill. The rider and her horse had completely vanished, leaving no tracks, and the usually brave wolfhound was whimpering and cowering.

Lieutenant Allison was soon joined by another officer, who teased him at first about the lovely lady who had given him the slip, but his kidding turned to amazement when he, too, failed to find any trace of the rider.

Back at the fort for dinner with the officers and their guests, Allison looked at all the ladies to make sure that none of them was his mystery woman. Then, risking the ridicule of everyone present, he told the assembled group of his eerie adventure. No one laughed, and the commanding officer explained to him, "Well, Allison, you have just seen the 'Laramie Ghost.' " Then he told her story.

In the old days when Fort Laramie had been a fur-trading post, a factor sent for his beautiful daughter who had been educated in the East. She was a skillful horsewoman, but her father nevertheless warned her not to ride out alone, and he ordered his assistants to make sure that she did not disobey him. But the young woman was headstrong and full of life, so one day when her father was away, and in spite of the protests of others at the fort, she galloped away on her favorite black horse. She was never seen alive again.

Her heartbroken father found no trace of her, and in the years to come, a legend grew among the Indians and traders in the region that every seven years the young girl's ghost would be seen riding down the old trail.

After hearing the story, Lieutenant Allison still did not want to believe that he had seen a ghost, so he sought out an elderly Indian woman who had been at the fort at the time of the disappearance of the factor's daughter. Imagine his amazement when she described what the young woman had been wearing: a long, dark green riding habit, a feathered hat, and a jewel-handled quirt!

Years later, Allison was riding a train through Wyoming when he overheard some cowboys on a depot platform talking about a rancher who had just seen the "Laramie Ghost." Unfortunately, before he could ask any questions, the train started up again.

Unlike the Lady in Green, who visits only at seven-year intervals, the spirit of a beautiful Indian maiden is said never to leave Fort Laramie. Born in 1848 to the great chief Spotted Tail, Brings Water spent some of her childhood years at Fort Leavenworth, where her father was incarcerated for leading his people in a "massacre" against Lieutenant John L. Gratton. The young girl was a great favorite with everyone she knew, and it was here that she developed her lifelong love both for white people and for military posts.

After Spotted Tail's release, the tribe moved to hunting grounds near Fort Laramie, where the tomboyish Brings Water dressed in buckskins like a man, and preferred riding horses and learning to use a gun and knife to the work that Indian women were expected to perform. All went well until her father was insulted by a drunken white man; from that time on, Spotted Tail vowed to have nothing to do with whites except to kill them.

Brings Water was so distraught by her father's decision that she slashed herself repeatedly with her knife, and threatened to commit suicide if he did not relent. He quickly gave in to her demands.

The child grew into a beautiful young woman, and when she was sixteen, she returned to Fort Laramie. She enjoyed sitting outside the store at the post, watching the soldiers in their fine uniforms, and she liked the company of the Confederate officers, who had the option of serving at western posts in lieu of going to prison.

After some time, Brings Water fell in love, but in some manner her heart was broken. Accounts differ as to whether her young man rejected her or was killed in a battle, or whether her father would not allow her to marry. She pined away, getting weaker and weaker until it was plain that she could not last long. Before her death, she begged her father to make peace with the whites, and she expressed a desire to be buried at Fort Laramie.

The young girl's coffin was draped in red cloth, and both Indians and whites honored her with gifts of clothing, money, and other items that she would need in the afterlife. Her two white ponies were killed, and their heads were nailed to the north posts and their tails to the south posts of her scaffold, erected so that she could be buried in the traditional Indian way. Under each pony's head, a container of water was placed to quench the animal's thirst on the journey to eternity.

During the funeral service for Brings Water, the clouds gathered and it began to sleet. The legend of the lovely Indian girl now maintains that her spirit still hovers over Fort Laramie, waiting for the man she loved, who joins her as they ride off together on the two white ponies.

In addition to Brings Water, could the spirits of others buried at Fort Laramie still be keeping watch there? Steve Caligiore's experience at the old burial ground near the ruins of the hospital suggests that at least some kind of strange power might still emanate from those graves.

A police dog belonging to an acquaintance of his was wearing a remote control device that emits a shock if the animal attempts to run too far from its owner. As the two men strolled nearby, the dog began howling and whimpering at the site of the unmarked graves. Without revealing that bodies were buried under their feet, Steve Caligiore watched his companion dowse the area with pieces of a wire coat hanger.

"He held a wire in each hand, and pretty soon those wires started to turn in toward him. Wherever the two met in the center, he marked the spot with a small rock; then he walked another three feet and did the same thing, and then six feet and did the same thing again. Before long, the patterns of the rocks clearly suggested a row of graves to him, so I told him that when the hospital was built, the workers apparently had to move the bodies to put up a wall."

Why did both the dog wearing the electronic device and the dowsing wires react so strongly to the presence of the graves? Were they actually sensitive to some kind of spiritual energy, or were they just affected by metal that may have been in the coffins?

The explanation for this phenomenon is as yet unknown, but Dr. Don Rickey has a theory about some of the other unusual happenings at Fort Laramie. He postulates that the "living history" experience may actually encourage spirits from the past to reach out to those who have symbolically stepped back into their time period. By dressing as they dressed, by acting as they acted, and by generally entering into the essence of their bygone age, we may seem reassuringly familiar to these earlier inhabitants of the fort, so that they want to make their presence known to us. If Dr. Rickey's hypothesis is correct, it is easy to see why the past never dies at Fort Laramie.

TO CATCH
A
THIEF

I f there is a prevailing lesson that collectors of ghost stories learn from the many and varied tales that come their way, it must be that the living risk losing peace of mind and sometimes even worse calamity if they disturb or dishonor the remains of the dead.

Warren Shipp* discovered this the hard way about forty years ago. Since he was part Indian himself, he was well acquainted with the traditional custom of the burial cave, in which a person's most prized material possessions are entombed along with his remains, so that they will continue to be of use to him in the afterlife.

It is unknown whether Warren had been present at this particular burial or had merely done some exploring on his own of the caves in the canyon at Dinwoodie, but the fact was that he knew of a very fine, practically new saddle that was being wasted on *this* plane of existence, even if its owner had taken it in spirit to the Happy Hunting Grounds!

The more Warren thought about the saddle, the more it bothered him to think of it lying uselessly in the cave alongside the dead man. Warren desperately needed a new saddle himself, and if he knew of one that was there for the taking, what was wrong with availing himself of it?

He rode to the cave in Bow Lake Creek Canyon, more fearful of the rattlesnakes that haunted the area than of any spirits of the dead. He began to feel nervous as he approached the mouth of the cave, but his greed for the prize it contained lured him inside. As soon as he saw what he had come for, Warren didn't linger, but grabbed the saddle, put it on his horse, mounted the steed, then galloped away.

Once out of the immediate area, Warren slowed his horse to a trot. For a few minutes he was content to feel the new saddle underneath him, and he congratulated himself on a job well done. Why should he feel guilty? It wasn't as if he had stolen anything, for how can one steal from the dead?

Just then he felt a small thud as if someone or something had landed on the saddle behind him, and a weak voice spoke into his ear.

"Take that saddle back!" the voice commanded. Warren's heart almost stopped and he whipped his horse into a gallop as if he could outride the thing perched behind him. But whatever it was leaned closer and spoke again in his ear. This time the voice was very loud and plain. "Take that saddle back!"

Without a second's hesitation, Warren whirled his horse around and galloped back to the cave. He uncinched the saddle, ran into the cave, and dropped it where he had found it.

He heard no more "orders" as he ran his poor, confused horse to the ranch of some friends. The woman noticed that he had been riding bareback at a pretty good clip when he pulled up to their door.

"When he asked to speak with my husband, he seemed very nervous and out of breath," she remembered. "He explained that he needed to borrow a saddle, because a job he wanted hinged upon his having one." Then Warren confessed the complete story of his attempted "theft."

"I know he believed he heard that voice," the woman said. "He's not one to tell lies."

Chances are, no longer was he one to steal the property from Indian burial caves, either!

THE DARK PRESENCE

O ne of the most terrifying supernatural encounters in the state began innocently enough in the early 1970s, when sisters Lois Dean and Diantha Summer moved their families into the old property on Spruce Street in the middle of Rawlins. The turn-of-the-century, two-story home with its carriage house converted into a duplex seemed the perfect place for the families to raise their growing brood. Lois, her husband, and six children took the big house, while Diantha and her two sons moved into one of the duplex apartments at the left and rear.

The families soon noticed that peculiar things were happening, but the phenomena seemed harmless enough at first. Lois and her husband heard mysterious scratching sounds that they attributed to a tree limb brushing against the house—until they discovered that no branches were close enough to do that. Then the lights kept turning off and on, especially in the garage and in a small bathroom downstairs.

"We thought the kids were leaving them on," Lois explained, "so we kept reminding them to turn them off. But as soon as they flipped the switch, the lights would come right back on. My husband finally had the house rewired, but that didn't stop it."

Other unexplained phenomena involved one of their oldest daughters, who habitually found the colors of her makeup blended together in a dresser drawer. She, too, accused the children, and believed in their innocence only after she had padlocked the door to her bedroom and found the colors run together, anyway. This daughter also noticed that when she practiced playing her drums, she would often hear her "tump de tump tump" perfectly repeated on one of the pipe vents leading out through the roof.

Doors were known to slam and then open back up by themselves, and closets that were opened would mysteriously spring shut again, as if someone were pulling on them from the inside. There were also the inexplicable cold spots that appeared even during the hottest summers, along with such a frightening atmosphere in the basement that nobody ever went down there alone.

"And sometimes when we were playing games," Diantha's son Mike Newberry remembered, "we would go to get a drink or something, and when we got back, the pieces would be missing from the game board. Other times, lamps would tip over by themselves, or doors would open before you got to them. We had two trunks stacked up, and the top one kept flying off by itself. And once, the boyfriend of one of my cousins was climbing through a window when something grabbed him by the shirt collar and threw him up against a wall into the room. When he finally got out of the house, he swore he'd never come back. And he never did!"

Mike recalled also that the family dog frequently wagged its tail at the presence of an invisible guest, and it often appeared to be watching somebody walk from one end of a room to the other.

It was Lois's six-year-old son Richard who finally gave a name to the ghost, however. "Two or three times a night I had to get up and cover him," Lois explained, "because he would kick off the blankets, curl up into a ball, and turn blue! But one night he told me, 'Don't worry, Mom. George covers me up.' So after that, we all called our playful ghost George."

Mike recalled that George's favorite trick seemed to be the raiding of the family medicine chest. "We thought maybe he had been the doctor who had owned the house before, because often we found the bathroom cabinet completely empty. Toothbrushes, combs, all the medicine that had been inside would be gone, and we'd find it later in odd places. I remember Richard and Alan coming home from school once and finding their toothbrushes under their beds!"

With so many children in the place, no one would have been surprised if they, rather than the ghost, had been moving things around. But this possibility was disproved one day when all the kids were in school and Lois was alone in the house.

"I had just gotten my cleaning supplies out from under the kitchen sink when I was interrupted," she said. "When I came back about an hour later, there in the crawl space was this whole mound of toothbrushes that the ghost had apparently dumped. They certainly hadn't been there an hour before. I just rolled my eyes and said, 'George, you're not funny!'"

The families came to believe that other entities besides George were sharing their living quarters. "For several months we had another ghost that the kids called both the Levi Man and the Streaker," Lois said, "because all they could see were a pair of Levis streaking by. You'd catch a glimpse of him out of the corner of your eye, and when you turned around, he would go by so fast that it was like looking at a speeded up film."

An unidentified, strong smell of perfume that traveled from room to room indicated the possible presence of a female ghost who was never seen, but the most convincing evidence that spirits really were inhabiting the house was captured both on audio tape and on a photographic negative.

"We took a tape recorder upstairs and left it on for an hour and a half," Mike said, "and then we listened to it all the way through. At the very end, we heard two very low voices that sounded like an echo, as if they were in a tunnel. One was definitely a man, but the other sounded to me like a child. The first one said, 'Here they come.' And then a tinnier-sounding voice answered, 'Let's go!' We even asked people we hardly knew to listen to the tape and tell us what they heard, and they all heard exactly the same thing."

Equally mysterious was the image of an upside down Christmas tree that appeared on the negative, peel-off part of a Polaroid snapshot. "It looks just like a Christmas tree, right down to its point, standing against one of the vents to the roof," Lois recalled. "And there was no such thing there at all. We never had a Christmas tree anywhere upstairs."

It was about this time that the innocent pranks blamed on George came to an end, and for some unknown reason, the feeling enveloping the two residences became more sinister. It became especially frightening to walk between the big house and the apartment in the rear.

"Since we all did a lot of going back and forth between the two places, it was easy for everyone to notice the change in atmosphere," said Diantha Summer. "First the kids started asking that the porch light be left on while they went back and forth at night. Then they wanted to be watched or accompanied, and more often than not, they ran the distance."

The adults were just as uncomfortable, Lois asserted. "Not because of anything we saw, or because of anything that happened, but we just had an ominous feeling that we were being watched, and always from the same area, from the direction of the old church next door. I can't explain what it was like, except to say that it kept building until it felt *thicker,* somehow, colder and thicker, and it even seemed to get darker in the space between the apartment and the house. And what made it seem so stupid was that there was no concrete reason for us to feel that way."

On the night when the evil presence seemed the most threatening, both Mike Newberry and Lois Dean had experiences they would prefer to forget. The sisters had withdrawn into the family room to discuss their fears that the mysterious evil, whatever it was, was advancing toward the house. Diantha vowed that the thing had to be stopped, so the sisters united in a prayer for protection.

"In the meantime," Diantha recalled, "the kids were growing excited at the prospect of getting what they called 'the old witch.' Because for some reason, we all agreed that the presence seemed female. The kids ran back and forth to the door, giggling and daring each other to go out, but we told them to stop, because it was a serious matter."

Mike, who was fourteen or fifteen at the time, probably has the clearest memory of what happened next. "My cousin Richard came in from the garage and said that something was in there," he remembered. "Well, I wanted to be the hero, so I opened up the back door to go out. I'd always been taught to recite the Lord's Prayer in scary situations, so I started saying, 'Our Father, Who art in Heaven.' But just as I got about halfway through, I suddenly forgot the words. I hesitated for maybe thirty seconds, trying to remember, when suddenly I felt two hands pick me up by the front of my shirt and throw me four or five feet up in the air and back into the kitchen, until I crashed into the refrigerator! The door was closed, and as I sailed through it, I broke off the latch."

Diantha, Lois, and Lois's daughter Pam were in the kitchen making sandwiches. They looked up to see Mike hurtling through the air, tangled up with Shawn, who had somehow collided with his brother outside and was also tumbling head over heels into the house.

"All we saw was a black shape, and then Shawn coming through the door backwards," said Lois. "He fell down, and Michael came flying inside. But he was headed in one direction one minute, and the next he was backwards in the air. They were both shouting hysterically that 'she' had attacked Mike and was going to kill them. We helped Mike up, and that's when we noticed that he had large red marks and welts on his chest, evidence that he had been scratched when he was picked up.

"Of course, all the children were frantic, and it was a long time before we got them calmed down. But I was furious, because the kids had been hurt and our home was being invaded. I saw the black shape head toward the garage, so I went outside to challenge it. I said, 'I don't care who you are—I'm not putting up with you coming into my home and hurting the kids!' As I went into the garage, I could see the black shape standing in the far corner. It's hard to describe, but it looked something like a nun's habit with the white removed from it. It was big, billowy, and dressed like a woman in something black and long.

"I kept screaming, 'I'm not afraid of you!' and I called it a few choice names. And then it started coming toward me, not like it was walking, but as if it were on wheels. It was just rolling smoothly toward me.

"Now it was night, we were in a dark garage, and the only illumination was from moonlight coming through the window. The shape was within a few feet of me when something black and cold started coming out of it, like strands or ribbons. Off of the thing, off of its clothing. And it started wrapping me with those strands, and I could feel their coldness. It started at my feet, not hard or pulling tight, but just a loose, cold wrapping. The strands looked like burning oil, like wisps or ragged streamers. I was rooted to the spot, and I cried out, 'Oh, my God!' and looked down at my feet. I couldn't move on my own, but it was the fear, not the wrapping, that stopped me. I was terrified of what might happen if the wrapping went much farther up my legs.

"And then I felt my sister grab me from behind and jerk me all the way back into the house. She had seen the shape, too," Lois said, and years later her voice still quakes when she remembers. "She got me safely inside, but I was just wiped out. Here I had been so furious that I thought I could lick anything, but this encounter nearly devastated me.

"I never did see a face, and I thank God for that, as well as for the fact that it never did get more than a few feet from me, except for those horrible streamers reaching out to trap me. After my sister pulled me into the house, we stayed up all night, praying hard, and we never did see that hideous thing again."

Did the combination of prayer and Lois's struggle with the mysterious adversary cause it to go away for good? While everyone I spoke with agreed that the atmosphere was less oppressive afterwards, they all were aware that something was still not right.

Several years after what Lois now half-jokingly refers to as "the main event," Mike Newberry left home, then moved back in later with his wife Traci. Neither of them liked living there, but it was rent-free in exchange for their keeping up the property. Traci's own childhood home had harbored a "friendly" ghost (see "Barney"), but she was depressed by the gloomy atmosphere on Spruce Street.

"It felt like someone was out to get us," she said, "or else to torment us until we left." Several times she heard the sounds of an infant crying, but upon checking on her own children, she always found them sleeping soundly. At night she occasionally glimpsed a shadowy figure darting into the bedroom, and the temperature was often subject to sudden change.

"Sometimes you would walk into a room and it would be comfortably warm, but if you left for a few seconds and then came back, it would be icy cold as if all the heat had been turned off for a long time," Traci said.

Mike and Traci eventually moved out, obviously with no regrets. "I'm glad I don't have anything to do with that house anymore," insisted Mike. "I wouldn't buy it if it was on sale for ten dollars!"

It seems odd that a place could be so haunted for so long without anyone ever knowing why. The only clue may be in the fact that the property sits next to what was formerly an old church.

Lois Dean recalled that her Aunt Garnet, born in 1900, often played in the carriage house as a child. "She told me that there had been a small graveyard to the right of the church, and when she was quite young, the bodies from it were exhumed and moved to the Rawlins cemetery. But there was talk that two bodies had been left behind."

Mike Newberry also talked with the woman who had lived in the house just before his family moved in, and she had heard the same story, including the fact that the bodies were left by mistake because the graves were not well marked.

The church and the house are still there, but the church has been gutted and converted into law offices. The house has also been completely remodeled, and the last Mike heard was that it had been put up for sale. Were all the renovations enough to put an end to the wanderings of some of Rawlins's most restless spirits? Or are they still waiting in the abandoned graveyard to torment the next inhabitants of the house on Spruce Street?

THE FRIENDLY PHANTOM
OF
FORT BRIDGER CEMETERY

F ort Bridger Cemetery in the southwest corner of the state is well over a hundred years old, but the ghost that groundskeeper Ramon Arthur became acquainted with is definitely a twentieth-century fellow.

Ramon began working summers at the cemetery in May 1987, and at the time of my first interview with him in December of that year, he had already seen, heard, or felt the presence of the ghost seven or eight times.

"The first time I saw him was the middle of June," he said. "I was cutting the grass along a row of shrubs when I looked up and saw this fellow walking along another row opposite me. He kept strolling along until he passed through an opening right behind me; then he came so close I could have reached out and touched him. I wondered what he wanted, so I shut my gas trimmers off and turned around. But I couldn't believe my eyes—there was nobody there!"

After searching the area without success, Ramon began to look for tracks in the grass, but the only ones he found were his own.

"That was the end of that sighting, and it was very brief. But I did have time to notice that he had on the whitest cowboy hat you ever saw. Not a great big one, but it had about a four-inch brim."

Ramon added that he could tell the apparition was of fairly recent times because of the clothes he wore. "You've seen those western suits with the jacket to the waist?" he asked. "That's the kind of coat it was, or a blue denim jacket, one of the two. I never did notice the lower part of his body, but I could tell that he moved pretty fast. And he was about six feet tall."

Since he went on to encounter the ghost so many times, it seems odd that Ramon never got a good look at its face. "There just wasn't a face there to see, that I ever noticed," he said, claiming that all he could make out was a head with no discernible features.

When he saw the ghost the second time, Ramon had just finished cleaning the grass from the bagger of his riding lawn mower. As he stood up, he saw the phantom standing about a hundred feet away, close to where he had been seen the first time.

"No sooner did I see him than he was gone again," said Ramon. "He just disappeared right into the shrubs."

The ghost made his presence felt more strongly during the next encounter. "My mower plugged up again, and when I had cleaned it, I tried to back up out of the way in order to shut the lid. But I couldn't. There was something holding me from behind. It gave me kind of a funny feeling, and when I turned around, there was that same white hat and blue jacket!

"Another time I was trimming underneath a heavy bed of lilacs, when I heard somebody walking up the gravel road nearby. People come into the cemetery all the time and want to ask me questions, so I stood up in order to be seen. I walked out to the place where the footsteps seemed to be coming from, but there was nobody there."

Ramon went back to work and heard the crunching on the gravel again. Once more he walked to the road to find nobody there. The third time he heard the noise, he stayed in place and kept working.

"The sound of walking eventually went past me, then died away. But I never saw anybody. It was just like an invisible person was passing by."

Except for the first time he saw the specter, Ramon has never been afraid; in fact, he came to view the ghost as a friend, especially after an experience in late August 1987.

"My tractor was stuck on some cement and I couldn't get it out. I was going to prop up one side of it with boards while I lifted the other, but then I decided to try once more without the props. Well, when I hoisted up my side, would you believe that the other one raised up by itself? Then the whole back end of that mower just lifted right up onto the front wheels and off the cement! It must have been that guy helping me," he said and laughed. "When it was all over, what could I say except 'Well, thanks!' "

Another time the ghost got into mischief by switching off the cemetery's sprinkler system. Ramon had set the pumps for heavy watering, and had started on some other work, when he looked up to see that his sprinklers had shut off.

"I went to check at the building where the pumps are, and I found that the pressure switches on the tanks had been turned off," he said. "I certainly hadn't done it, and there was nobody there but me that day."

On another occasion, when some workers were laying blacktop for the pumphouse, Ramon saw the ghost walk right around the corner and into the building. The workers were apparently at the wrong angle to see him, and Ramon explained, "I never told them about him, either. I was afraid they'd leave!"

Ramon's most puzzling experience was seeing the ghost at his own home about a mile from the cemetery. "One night I was weeding the vegetable garden, and I happened to look up in time to see him walk into my greenhouse," he said. "I don't know how he got there, or why he came. Maybe he got in the car and rode home with me."

Ramon Arthur had no idea who his phantom friend was until the spring of 1988, when he saw him for what he believes may have been the last time. Just before Memorial Day, he was weeding a grave when he suddenly sensed the familiar presence. Not wanting to glance up quickly and scare the ghost away as he had done in previous encounters, Ramon kept his head down, continuing his work and trying not to stare too obviously at the pair of shiny black boots planted ten feet in front of him.

Ramon had never before seen anything but the hat and jacket of the ghost, but somehow he knew that this being in the black boots was his old friend. This silent communion continued for three or four minutes, and was broken only when Ramon was forced to lift up his head to move to another grave. As soon as he did so, the apparition vanished.

This was the only sighting Ramon witnessed during the 1988 spring and summer season, and after wondering about the identity of the specter for so long, he believes he may have found the answer in a man in his sixties who died shortly before Memorial Day 1987. It was that same month that Ramon began his work as groundskeeper and experienced his first encounter with the ghost. Then, in June 1988, the man's widow also died, and after she was buried, Ramon saw no more of the apparition.

"Now I think maybe he was just hanging around here waiting for her," he said, "because he knew she was going to be joining him soon. But they had both lived hard lives, and they had both been sick. They weren't exactly friends of mine, but I knew who they were."

It seems ironic that the Fort Bridger cemetery, formerly an old military burial ground, should feature such a prosaic sort of twentieth-century ghost when it could be swarming with the spirits of all those soldiers from Wyoming's romantic past. And it is also odd that Ramon Arthur should be visited by the ghost of a man he hardly knew, when so many of his own family members have been laid to rest in the cemetery he tends. Even though his mother, father, brother, sister, grandmother, uncles, and other relatives are buried there, Ramon was sure from the outset that the ghost was none of these.

But whatever the spook's identity, Ramon Arthur, who has lived all of his more than fifty years in Fort Bridger, finds nothing scary in the notion of supernatural visitations. After his mother died, he remembers his father telling him from time to time, "Well, Minnie just stopped in to see me a little while ago." And though she never said anything to Ramon's father, she sat in a favorite chair and comforted him by her presence.

With such a positive introduction to the concept of spirits, it's no wonder that Ramon Arthur had come to regard the cemetery ghost as a special friend, one that he is certain to miss.

THE HOUSE
NOBODY
WANTS

When succeeding groups of occupants don't stay in a particular dwelling for more than a few weeks or months, it's a good guess that there might be something a little peculiar about the place. In 1980, Sandra Eno and her children moved away from their small brick home on Avon Street in Sheridan, and in the nine years since then, no one has lived in the house for more than a short period of time. Sandra's story of her experiences there might explain why.

The family moved into the house on a summer day in the late 1970s, and the ghostly manifestations began the very first week. While she was in her bedroom, Sandra heard the unmistakable sounds of a rocking chair creaking back and forth over the floor upstairs, even though no such item of furniture was in the house. "There were just some things for the kids up there, and they hadn't even moved into their rooms yet," she explained. "I heard the rocking noise several times, and when I finally went to check, I saw that there was nothing up there that could be causing it. I didn't think too much of it at the time, though. I've had lots of experiences with ghosts and various spirits, and they don't frighten me. But this rocking reoccurred even after my sons had moved in, and I realized that the noise seemed to be coming from one of their rooms. Whenever I went to check, I could still hear it, but I never saw anything, and my sons would always be fast asleep. It was a little weird, but I wasn't scared, because the dogs and cats never got upset.

"Then other things started happening. The kitchen cupboard doors would come open, even the ones that were so high that none of us could reach them. I made a point of making sure that they were all closed every night, but the next morning they would be open again. And it would be different cupboard doors, sometimes one and then another. It finally got so bad that you couldn't leave the room without a door opening up!

"It was about this time that I began to sense that our family was not alone. I usually felt the presence in the dining room, and I knew from the start that it was female. As I learned more about the history of the place, I came to believe that our spirit was the woman who had lived here before the people from whom we had bought the house. I began to feel her presence more and more often, and several times that first winter, the back door would come open, even though we always shut it. It wasn't the kind of door that could blow open, either, because it fit the frame snugly and the latch worked perfectly."

Sandra's daughter Michelle twice heard the sound of footsteps going up a staircase that was located behind her bedroom. At the time, she and her mother were alone in the house, and her mother was asleep in her room. At other times, both of them would catch a glimpse of something out of the corners of their eyes, but when they turned to look, nothing was ever there.

"I was getting a little perturbed by all this," Sandra continued. "But then, in the spring when I was cleaning up the yard, I discovered bulbs and flowers planted everywhere. My neighbor told me that Lottie, the woman I believed to be our ghost, had been an avid gardener whose pride and joy were the trees and flowers she tended so carefully every year. But each time she went to visit her sister, her mean-spirited husband would cut down one of her fruit trees. Apparently he was a very nasty person, always angry and always killing Lottie's flowers and doing other things to make her unhappy. So you can see that the two of them must have lived miserable lives. They were both elderly when they died, Lottie first, and then her husband, who was killed when he drove his car into Big Goose Creek. I guess no one knew whether he committed suicide or had an accident.

"Finding the bulbs and hearing about Lottie's life made me feel very close to her, so I started talking to her when I was in the house by myself. Eventually, I could see a kind of shimmering light, usually around the bay window, and I felt a very warm, nice feeling. But

I could tell that something was worrying her, and that she wanted to communicate with me.

"Not long afterwards, the people from whom we had bought the house returned for a visit. For some reason, when they moved out, they had taken a family Bible that had belonged to Lottie. I thought it odd that they had taken it, and that they were now bringing it back. But I had the feeling that having the Bible again made Lottie very happy, and I left it in the house for her when we finally moved. And as soon as the Bible had been returned, the cupboard doors didn't open up by themselves so often.

"While I liked having Lottie around, I never did like the house itself. And other things were beginning to go wrong for our family, so we decided to leave Wyoming. We put the house up for sale, but we absolutely could not sell it. People would make offers and then retract them; it was very frustrating. The back door started opening up again, and the kitchen cupboard doors were doing the same thing.

"I knew that Lottie didn't want us to leave, and we weren't having any luck selling the house, so we took it off the market. But problems with health and finances made us realize that we had to leave, so I put the house up for sale again. This time, I knew I had to explain things to Lottie; so one night when I knew she was there, I told her, 'You have to let us go! You have to let us sell this house.' I talked to her for a long time, telling her firmly that we were going to move and that she had to release her hold over us. And the house sold very soon after that.

"I know she was glad when we lived with her," Sandra said. "She was happy having a family, since her own life with her husband had been so sad. I often felt that she was upstairs, watching over my sons, and goodness knows they needed it! They admitted that sometimes they, too, felt that she was looking after them."

Surely a ghost as loving and protective as Lottie would like to have a new family to look after, so why has she made life so difficult for all those who have moved into the house on Avon Street over the last nine years? Does she think she can get Sandra's family to come back if she keeps misbehaving, or is she just very choosy about whom she allows to live with her? If that is the case, one can only hope that she will soon find another family as deserving of her care.

WYOMING
GHOST
LIGHTS

O ne of the weirdest phenomena in the state of Wyoming undoubtedly has a natural explanation. The only problem is that nobody knows for sure what it is!

Eerie, globular "ghost lights," as they are called, are hardly unique to the Cowboy State. Many regions of the United States, and, in fact, other parts of the world, have their own stories about the unexplained balls of illumination that sometimes appear in the nighttime sky, then float, often just a few feet from the ground, until they disappear. Many scientists who have studied the phenomenon believe that the glowing spheres are produced by natural gas escaping from the ground, while others believe them to have an electromagnetic cause. Whatever their origin, ghost lights are certainly one of the best documented of all mysterious occurrences, as they have frequently been photographed; on Halloween night 1988, the most famous ones in the country, those in Marfa, Texas, were even filmed for a segment of the *CBS Evening News with Dan Rather.*

Peter Van Zandt filed the report from the Big Bend country of southwest Texas, where the strange orbs of light have puzzled onlookers for generations. A special night camera filmed the ghost lights as they drifted over the desert floor, sometimes splitting into two parts before the delighted eyes of the watchers who had come for the special Halloween showing.

Although they are not as well known, the ghost lights in Wyoming are much the same as those in Texas or anywhere else. Loren Coleman in his book *Mysterious America* lists locations of the spook lights from around the nation (none of which are in Wyoming, however), and he defines them as "mysterious, usually mobile globes of illumination seemingly attached to, and appearing periodically at specific locations" (Boston: Faber and Faber, 1983, 261). In the companion book, *Curious Encounters*, Coleman goes on to mention that the growing body of scholarship on the subject has demonstrated "that phenomenon's unique attraction to streams, groves of trees, roads, certain fields, mountains, and railroads" (Boston: Faber and Faber, 1985, 81-82).

Consider now the stories of two women who are well acquainted with some Wyoming ghost lights that have been appearing at least since the beginning of the twentieth century. Billie Jean Beaton, a former teacher, repeatedly saw the lights near the Salt Creek Oil Field when she lived on a ranch in the vicinity.

"Whenever I saw it, it looked like a single car headlight, and it seemed to glide, following the contours of the land," she said. "Sometimes it would change from a bright yellow to a kind of golden color, and it seemed to be most prevalent on the outskirts of the oil field, about thirty miles north of Casper. Back in the early days, there were lots of range people from Scotland and Ireland who brought in livestock of all kinds, principally sheep. Some of these folks were very superstitious, and most of the early stories about the lights circulated among them and the ranchers living in areas outside the oil field. The lights were really well known from the early 1900s through the 1960s, but they aren't reported as often today, probably because fewer people are living on the range.

"I knew a rancher who lived in the area west of the oil field. He was crippled from polio, and he usually slept only three or four hours a night. We used to help him with his work, and he often told us about sitting up and watching this light as it glided along. It never seemed to stay in one place for any length of time, and it just sort of floated at a certain distance above the ground. He saw it mainly on clear, fairly cool nights, in all seasons.

"The herders who saw it claimed that it would float in right around their sheep wagons, and many of them were afraid to go out at night because of all the stories they had concocted about the lights being lanterns carried by the spirits of their dead friends. Maybe some of the herders had guilty consciences—I don't know about that! But

I guess they thought someone was after them," Billie Jean said with a laugh.

"Often, people who hadn't heard of the light would come up to haul hay to our ranch," she continued. "I remember a fellow who came in from work one evening. We hadn't seen each other for a long time, but he didn't even say hello. He just blurted out, 'Have you ever heard of the light?' I told him I had and smiled, but that man must have been scared to death, as pale and quiet as he was the rest of the evening. Seeing the light seemed to affect a lot of people that way.

"My own closest experience with it occurred on a moonlit night when I was driving back from a school function in Midwest, Wyoming," Billie Jean continued. "With me were my three children and another lady, who had two children of her own. We were probably about ten miles west of the oil field, on the Shepperson Ranch Road, which led only to the ranch and then dead-ended, so it never had much traffic. Suddenly I saw this light traveling toward us. At first I thought that it was our husbands, coming to meet us in our car after becoming worried that we'd been gone too long. But whatever it was kept coming, and as it drew closer, I could see that it was only a single light. As I was up on a hill, I decided to pull off the road to see whether it would pass by. I turned off the car lights and we waited; the light kept coming toward us until it moved under the bluff of a hill; then it didn't come any closer, and we didn't see it anymore.

"I joked with my friend that we'd just seen the ghost light, but I decided that it really must have been our husbands, who had probably seen our lights from a long way off and had turned around and headed back to the ranch. I was so sure of what had happened that the minute I got home, I went over and touched the radiator of my husband's car, knowing that it would still be warm if he had just returned. But it was as cold as could be, and both our husbands were in bed, sound asleep.

"The lady who had been riding with me was so stunned by the experience that she never would admit that we had seen the ghost light. I couldn't understand her acting that way, because she was an intelligent woman.

"My son still lives in that area, and he says he has seen the light at a distance several times in the last two years. And my husband told me that quite a long time ago, lots of people talked about having seen a light in the direction of Teapot Creek."

Like Billie Jean Beaton, Eula Lee Petersen has also seen the light many times, at least a hundred by her estimation. But unlike many of those who witnessed the spectacle, Eula Lee has never been afraid. "You could tell by the way it traveled that it wasn't anything that was going to hurt you. It looked just like a ball of fire in the shape of a balloon a foot or two across, and the light was often reddish or bluish. I always saw it at dusk, but never when the moon was up. Because of the way it bounced along ridges, people said it was somebody carrying a lantern.

"Lots of people around Salt Creek and Dugout Creek said that it was the ghost of an Irishman named O'Rourke*," she explained. "Back in the 1920s, my first husband, Chris Jensen, had gone to town for a few days to take care of some business; Mrs. O'Rourke* had also gone, so when Chris returned, he gave her a ride home. When they reached her place, it was dark; and because they didn't see a light inside, Chris thought he had better go in with her to make sure that everything was all right. When they went in, they found Mr. O'Rourke dead. Apparently he had just sat down to the table and keeled over with a heart attack.

"After that, the Irish ranchers and settlers said that the light was really O'Rourke packing a lantern as he traveled across the hills. But, of course, it's probably just caused by escaping gas which follows the natural breaks of the land. At least that's what an old friend from the Colorado Bureau of Mines believed. I told him once that I had tried to catch the light two or three times, and he just grinned at me and said, 'And you never could, could you?'

"As I remember it, it would suddenly appear, and then it would move about as fast as you could walk, sometimes covering as much as a ten-mile area. It would stay in the sky for about an hour; then it would drop over another hill and be gone from sight. I never got closer than a quarter of a mile away. It seemed like the faster you walked toward it, the faster it moved away."

Eula Lee's first husband, Chris Jensen, as well as her second, Stanley Petersen, both saw ghost lights frequently when they homesteaded in the area. "In fact," Eula Lee insists, "just about anybody who ever lived in that vicinity saw the lights. And since there is quite a lot of natural gas as well as oil there, it probably does have something to do with their formation."

This is a definite possibility, but a New Jersey research group called Vestigia has developed another theory based upon its investigation of a ghost light site in that state. In the organization's newsletter, Dr. C. Louis Wiedemann explained that the light would "bob and sway from side to side in the manner of a swinging lantern, and when approached, it vanishes, sometimes reappearing at a distant point." This particular light always appeared on or near railroad tracks, as do many others around the world. Vestigia therefore postulated that ghost lights may be the result of "piezoelectric" effects produced by the squeezing of certain minerals (such as quartz) during earth movements and small earthquakes. The accumulation and subsequent discharge of the resulting electrical buildup through the metal train tracks could then produce the phenomenon known as ghost lights (*Curious Encounters*, 83-84).

While the Wyoming ghost lights discussed here do not follow railroad tracks, they do follow roads, as well as the natural contours of the land; so is it possible that these manmade and natural structures are also involved in creating piezoelectric effects? A 1941 account of another Wyoming ghost light suggests that roads, at least, may be instrumental in producing the strange phenomenon. In the state Writer's Program's *Wyoming: A Guide to Its History, Highways, and People* (New York: Oxford University, 221), the following appears: "Right from Newcastle on the unimproved Morrissey Road to the Ghost Light Area, 3 *m*. Strange vivid lights are said to roll over the ground here like tumbleweeds. Some motorists have reported driving their cars off the road to avoid hitting them."

Whatever ghost lights are, it is clear that they are a separate occurrence from ball lightning and will-o-the-wisps, other, perhaps related phenomena for which scientists are also seeking explanations. Eventually, humankind will surely unlock the secrets to these and other mysteries of what is now deemed "the supernatural," but might it not be more intriguing to leave them in the realm of magic?

BARNEY

When Marilyn Mills, her husband, and four daughters moved into the old house west of Rawlins in 1968, it didn't take them long to learn that there was something peculiar about their new home.

On their first night they kept hearing the scraping of branches against the windows, and it wasn't until they went to chop the offending bushes down next morning that they discovered there weren't any! And on a chilly April day not long afterwards, they heard a pitiful scratching at the back door.

"When we went to see what it was," Marilyn recalled, "there was this ancient Norwegian elkhound, so feeble it could barely drag itself up the back steps to get to the door. It looked us over carefully and then just sat down on the porch. The last owner of the place, a banker named Barney who had died a year or two before, had had a dog of this breed that had since been adopted by a family in Rawlins. So, even though it was cold and sleeting, we figured the poor thing had wandered the three miles from town to get back to its old home. I telephoned the new owners, but they said it couldn't have been Barney's dog, because it had just died.

"You can imagine the funny feeling that bit of news gave me! And when we went to check whether the dog on our doorstep had any identification, it was gone. We never saw it again, although we called and looked for it a long time. The whole episode sent chills up my spine, and it set the stage for everything that was to follow."

It wasn't long before the family was plagued by strange malfunctions of the electrical system. "When we moved in," Marilyn explained, "the electrical circuits were so faulty that we just removed everything, even pulling wires out of the walls as we tore them down. But in one of the rooms where we were sleeping during the renovation, a lightbulb kept turning on and off by itself, even though the electricity wasn't hooked up. And once when we were gone, we had a young boy staying at the house to feed the livestock. He was lying in bed watching TV with all the lights off, and suddenly, every light in the house came on, scaring the heck out of him.

"At other times, the radio would turn itself on when it wasn't even plugged in. Our ghost was also especially fond of a music box that my mother had brought the kids from Switzerland. Very few nights went by that one of us didn't wake up to the sound of its playing. Even if we let the mechanism run down, it wouldn't be long before the tune would start up again. Once I took the music box and put it in our bedroom, thinking that the ghost wouldn't dare to come in there to play it, but he did. I can't remember ever hearing the sounds of its being wound up, but it would continue to play, nevertheless."

Marilyn's former mother-in-law, Kate Belmain, heard the girls talking about their ghost, whom they believed to be Barney, the former resident. Initially she thought that they were just having fun, but after one unexplainable incident, she, too, became a believer.

"Whenever I went to visit," Kate remembered, "I always slept in the south bedroom, which was converted from the old entrance to the place. And I'm sure that Barney used to use it quite a lot. This one night I went to bed early, and I took with me a white toy poodle pup named Missy that I had given to my daughter. The dog barks a lot, and I thought that if I let her sleep on the end of my bed, she wouldn't bother anyone.

"Sometime in the middle of the night, the light suddenly came on. I sat up in bed and saw that Missy was shivering and whimpering, and I wondered what was wrong. I looked around to see if someone were in the room, but we were alone. My first thought was that the girls were playing tricks, but if that had been the case, Missy wouldn't have acted the way she did, because she knew them. So I settled her down and turned the light out and went back to sleep. But then it occurred again. The same thing. The light came on, and Missy was shivering and afraid. That time, I held her close to me, glad of her company even if she was just a little pup! One really odd thing was that even though the switch was in the off position, the light had come on, anyway. I flipped the switch again to turn the light off, and there were no more occurrences that night.

"In discussing the episode with Marilyn the next morning, I decided that nobody but Barney could have made the lights come on like that, and nothing else could have made Missy act the way she did. The experience made me a little shaky, but I never felt that I was going to be harmed in any way. I think Barney was probably just lonely and was trying to get some attention."

Marilyn's mother, Cora May Ekdahl, was also skeptical about supernatural phenomena, until she, too, encountered something out of the ordinary. "This particular time," she said, "I was babysitting my daughter's children, who were sleeping in the basement bedroom directly under the living room. I went down to be with them, but I had not gone to sleep. Suddenly, I heard the rocking of an old chair on the wood floor above, even though no one should have been upstairs. It rocked for a few minutes; then I heard a car drive up outside, and a whole bunch of people got out, laughing and talking gaily as if they were going to a party. The chair stopped rocking, and I heard someone walk across the floor and open the door.

"Thinking the kids might have returned, I went up to check, but there was no one there. Everything was in place and the door was locked. I never heard anything more, but I did very little sleeping that night."

Cora wondered whether the sounds she heard could have been leftover psychic impressions of the time when the house was a luxurious country club in the 1920s. In its heyday, it often served as the setting for elegant festivities, until bankruptcy forced its closure during Prohibition. After that time, the property degenerated into a bar, a dance hall, and a trysting spot for teenagers, until Barney bought it and made it his residence in the late 1940s. He intended to restore the building to something of its former purpose and grandeur, but died at home of a heart attack before he was able to realize his ambitions.

Could that be the reason why his spirit seemed to take such an interest in the remodeling done by Marilyn and her family? They don't discount the possibility, especially since the last mysterious phenomena took place in 1973, the year the renovations were completed.

"It seemed as though every time we finished fixing up a room, the ghost would leave it," Marilyn said. "And then he'd go on to other rooms, and as soon as we finished those, he would disappear from them, also."

But Barney wasn't the only one interested in what was being done to the old place. Many townspeople also dropped in out of curiosity to see the remodeling as it occurred. "During one couple's visit, we were standing in the kitchen, discussing and making fun of the many grand schemes that Barney had had for the property," Marilyn said. "All of a sudden, it sounded like a huge dog was growling at us somewhere in the room. We turned around and looked, but there was no dog to be found, my own being outside.

"Another time, Barney's nephew was visiting, and I was taking a break from painting the ceiling in what had been the ballroom. I had spread newspapers all over the floor, and we were sitting at the dining room table, again criticizing some of the things that Barney had wanted to do to the place. No sooner had we started to ridicule his plans than we heard angry footsteps stomping across the floor over those newspapers! We immediately got up to see who had done it, but there wasn't anybody else in the house."

Besides displaying his bad temper, however, Barney never did anything more harmful than stealing the children's homework, according to the youngest daughter, Traci Newberry. She explained, "We found it was a lot easier just to say we had forgotten to do it than to tell the teachers what had really happened. And usually the next day, it would show up someplace new in the house."

Indeed, most of the time Barney was considered to be a family friend and welcome companion, not a vengeful phantom to be feared. "In no way did we ever feel threatened by our ghost," Marilyn explained. "He was even a reassuring presence at times. When the kids were out here by themselves and heard a funny noise, they would just shrug it off as evidence that Barney was around. They were actually less scared than they would have been if they *hadn't* had a friendly ghost to blame those sounds on!"

Several times, in fact, Barney apparently acted as a kind of babysitter. "I often took my oldest daughter to my mother's house," Traci recalled, "and we always put her rocking bassinet in the bathroom, because it was the warmest place in the house. Jessica was very sickly as a baby, and Mom and I would take turns staying up with her all night. On several occasions when both of us were out of the bathroom, we'd hear a cry, and we'd return to find the bassinet gently rocking back and forth as if somebody were pushing it. The minute that we walked in, it would gradually begin slowing down, and the baby would soon be asleep again."

Marilyn Mills actually met Barney a few times when she was a child, when she occasionally rented horses from him to ride. She never knew him well during his lifetime, but the relationship she and her family have had with him after his death has resulted in their having mixed feelings now that he has apparently left them in peace.

"He was very friendly, and he was our explanation for things that went bump in the night," Marilyn said. "Sometimes we kind of miss him!"

THE GHOST
OF
ST. MARK'S
BELL TOWER

T he entity who haunts the bell tower of St. Mark's Episcopal Church in Cheyenne must be the only ghost in the state with a special room built exclusively for his use. Passersby on the corner of Nineteenth and Central can look up to see the Gothic windows that frame the spirit's private chamber; and inside, the hardwood maple floor and beautifully plastered walls set a tone of elegance that would delight any occupant, phantom or otherwise. Little has changed since the room's construction, although a chandelier once suspended from the ceiling has been removed.

Reporter Brad Hamilton's story in the *Wyoming State Tribune*, dated October 21, 1979, reveals how the ghost came to inhabit the room right below the carillon bells. The original St. Mark's, constructed in 1868, was the first church building in the state of Wyoming. As the congregation grew, it needed a bigger structure, so one was started in 1886. This new St. Mark's was to be a replica of England's Stoke Poges Church, made famous by Thomas Gray's "Elegy Written in a Country Churchyard." The only problem was that few people on the western frontier had the necessary skills to copy the stone work of the English church, but that obstacle was overcome when two Swedish immigrants were found to construct the tower and steeple.

The Swedes laid a foundation fifteen feet deep; then they began building the four-foot-wide circular walls required to support the heavy tower, tapering them gradually as they rose toward the sky. The construction seemed to be progressing nicely, with the man on the ground using a horse-drawn hoist to lift the heavy stone blocks to his fellow worker, who then fit them into place.

But one day when the massive tower stood forty feet high, one of the stonemasons failed to arrive at the site. The second man seemed unaccountably edgy before he, too, disappeared. Because no one else in the area had the expertise to work with the stone, there was nothing to do but to roof over the unfinished tower.

A ground-level room in the structure was made ready for Dr. George C. Rafter, the elderly, white-bearded rector of St. Mark's, who used it for his private study. Not long after he moved into the room, he reported hearing unexplained noises, such as tiny hammerings in the walls, and muffled voices from overhead. He had the attic checked to make sure that no one was hiding there, but it was found to be empty. After Dr. Rafter's resignation in 1904, his study was walled off and a pipe organ was installed in the room, which adjoined the chancel of the church.

The work on the tower was not resumed until 1927, however, and the new plans were to build a bell tower instead of a high steeple. The tower was erected to a height of sixty feet, and eleven carillon bells weighing nearly twenty tons were put into place. But this time the work did not go smoothly. The men on the job complained constantly of unspecified spooky occurrences, and were so upset that they actually halted construction several times.

They finally hit upon a possible solution. If the ghost could have his own room in the tower, perhaps he would be happier and, thus appeased, would allow them to complete their work. They broached the subject to the rector, the Reverend Charles Bennett, who, after much persuasion, reluctantly agreed to their request. With an eighty-five-foot open spiral staircase from the basement as the only means of entrance, the beautifully finished chamber was ever thereafter referred to as the "ghost room." Its remote location and difficulty of access insured that the spirit would always have his privacy.

In the years since then, many people have reported a variety of psychic phenomena throughout the church, ranging from the sighting of apparitions to the hearing of voices, many of them referring to a body entombed in the walls. It was not until 1966, when current rector Eugene Todd was summoned to Denver to hear the fascinating story of a nursing home patient, that the meaning of the voices was made clear.

The elderly man told the priest about his early days in South America, when he had known a Swedish stonemason who had once built part of the bell tower at St. Mark's. The mason confessed that his companion had been killed instantly in a fall from the tower, and that he himself had panicked for fear of being accused of murder and deported to Sweden. Not knowing what else to do, he curled his co-worker's corpse around the inside of one of the four-foot circular walls, then filled the wall with cement before building it up with stones on both sides. Still nervous, the surviving stonemason hurriedly departed Cheyenne for South America, where he lived the rest of his life. The hasty burial of his fellow worker continued to nag at his conscience, however, and he was anxious for the truth to be revealed after his death.

According to the *Tribune* article, the Reverend Todd has no interest in locating the stonemason's body for reburial. "That tower ghost has never had it so good," he maintained. "He's got a private chamber suite for a permanent residence, he can and does play the large carillons whenever he wishes, and once a year hundreds of people make their pilgrimage up the spiral staircase to be received and entertained as his guests.

"Besides, morticians tell me that his entombment in cement would totally have mummified his body by now. The ghost can proudly boast, in a Swedish accent, that his body literally is part of the foundation of this historical church. Burial in a cemetery would be a real 'put down' to him now."

Ten years after the article was written, the ghost still enjoys his private chamber and he still plays the carillons from time to time, but, sadly, he no longer entertains visitors each Halloween.

"It used to be a fun thing to do," Eugene Todd told me. "It was a big community event, and the young people especially enjoyed it. But then the story received coverage in the national press, and the producers of a California television show offered several times to fly me to their studio to talk about the ghost. I always declined, but by then, all the publicity had done its damage, anyway. The story had gotten changed into something evil and Satanic, and no one in the church wanted any part of that. We even got phone calls from exorcists, who were going to come and rid us of our ghost; so because of all this adverse attention, we quit giving the tours."

Much of the bad publicity resulted from one Halloween several years ago when a Cheyenne radio station invited well-known Denver psychic and talk show host Lou Wright to spend the night broadcasting with a deejay up in the tower.

"I thought the whole thing was a joke at first, because radio stations often do silly things to boost their ratings; and besides being a psychic, I'm a skeptic," Lou confessed. "But I agreed to come, and the radio station paid for my flight. I was late getting into Cheyenne, so I was taken straight to the station, and as we drove by a church, I said, 'Oh, my God, is *that* it?' And I was told that it was. I had the feeling even then that St. Mark's was definitely haunted.

"We picked up the necessary broadcasting equipment from the radio station and returned to the church, where the rector met us. At that time, I knew nothing of the history of the building, but halfway up the stairs leading to the bell tower, I suddenly froze with a peculiar, frightened feeling.

"I told the priest how I felt," Lou explained, "and he handed me an article about the stonemason, saying that it might explain my reaction. I also told him that I had received the impression of a couple of spirits, and he asked me to describe them."

Eugene Todd still remembers one of Lou's descriptions, that of an old, white-haired bachelor who walked with a cane. "It was very obvious to whom she was referring," he said, "because she described the original rector, George Rafter, exactly as he was. That surprised me, since she had no way of knowing about him."

The deejay brought Lou a fast-food dinner; then the two of them settled down for their night in the "ghost room." Before the couple were locked alone in the church (to prevent anyone getting in or out), the lights and power to the rest of the building were turned off.

Lou and the deejay began their broadcast, first sitting at the window looking out over the graveyard, where the psychic immediately reported seeing "little white balls of light that could have been energy from spirits." For better transmission, however, the two moved to the window looking out over the street, where they waved to drivers honking their horns.

"At first, it seemed like just another fun Halloween night, but after a while, we both noticed mysterious shadows under the door. And then we saw these little blue lights moving up the stairway to the bell tower," Lou recalled. "I had seen them earlier when I was talking with the rector, and he told me that they might be the spirits of little children who used to go up to ring the bells.

"But then some really frightening phenomena began to occur," Lou continued, "things that I would just as soon forget. I know it sounds unbelievable, but a jelly-like substance started oozing from the baseboards, and the bells in the tower began to ring! And both the deejay and I heard a man's voice warning us, 'Get out while you still have your mind!'

"Naturally, we had no desire to stay up there any longer! The bells were suddenly so loud that we couldn't hear ourselves think, and the deejay pleaded over the radio for someone to get us out of that room. Fortunately, the station manager heard us and contacted the rector, and both of them came to free us within fifteen minutes. My feet never hit the stairs—I was out of that church like a bullet!

"Another strange thing is that the bells went off again about twenty minutes after we left," Lou added, "and when the police went up into the tower, they found no footprints on the dusty floor to indicate that anyone had been up there!

"I wouldn't go into that church again for any amount of money," she insisted, "but I called a reporter from *The National Enquirer* who came to talk with the rector. When the priest was called away to the phone, the reporter noticed a parishioner sitting in one of the pews, so he walked over to question him. But just as the reporter got to within a few feet of him, the seated man vanished into thin air!

"Now, don't get me wrong; I don't think that the spirits at St. Mark's are evil," Lou explained. "They just don't want any notoriety. They were probably upset that we were taking them so lightly, that we were disturbing their peace and quiet to do such a dumb thing. Since then, a radio station in Denver has tried to get me to broadcast from haunted houses, but I'll never do anything like that again. I've never felt so terrified in my life!"

The Reverend Todd is equally convinced that spirits reside in the building, but unlike Lou Wright, he seems to derive comfort from their presence. "I've always said that if there is a ghost, it certainly is a friendly one, and I'm not worried about it. In fact, when people ask me whether the church is haunted," he explained, "I say that it is filled with the spirits of all the men, women, and children who have worshipped, been baptized, married, or buried from here. The atmosphere is permeated with the good and bad memories of one hundred and twenty years, so it would be very sad if people *didn't* feel something when they came inside this gorgeous old church. After all, a lot of exciting, beautiful, and even historical things have happened in it.

"And yes, I'm sure that the spirits of George Rafter and the stonemason are here, along with the spirits of all the others," the Reverend Todd said. "And I hope that my spirit, too, will linger here after I'm gone."

There are certainly less pleasant places for spirits to linger, and one can't help but feel that even the solitary ghost in the bell tower wouldn't mind foregoing some of his privacy to be in such good company!

Fort Laramie's surgeon's quarters, where participants in the "living history" program once observed light from a ghostly lantern. See "The Past Never Dies at Fort Laramie."

The eerie manifestations inside this house west of Rawlins began as soon as Marilyn Mills's family moved in. See "Barney."

Leigh and Virgil Wilson's home in Sheridan was troubled by a host of supernatural phenomena, ranging from appartitions to shaking beds to strange odors. See "How to Reform a Haunted House."

Ted Louie riding in a parade in Thermopolis. See "The Shoshone Bar is Haunted." *Photo courtesy of Cathryn Poague.*

Chief Black Foot (second from left) holding the tomahawk that served as a sign between him and a Virginia pyschic. See "The Extraordinary Tale of Chief Black Foot." *Photo courtesy of Smithsonian Institution Photo No. 3418.*

St. Mark's Episcopal Church in Cheyenne, originally
intended to be a replica of England's Stoke Poges
Church. See "The Ghost of St. Mark's Bell Tower."

A harvest moon rises over the Ferris Mansion of Rawlins. See "Ghosts of
the Ferris Mansion." *Photo taken and supplied by Ted Schnell.*

Looking down the rows of officers' quarters as they appeared from 1913-1918. See "The Haunting of F.E. Warren Air Force Base." *Photo courtesy of the Wyoming State Archives, Museums and Historical Department.*

TO BID
YOU
FAREWELL

ick Weathermon isn't the sort of person who is overly concerned with matters of the supernatural. Yet in the late summer of 1972, he had an experience that can hardly be explained in any other way.

He was working as a maintenance man up at Pahaska on the North Fork, just east of Yellowstone Park. By September, only four or five of the normal summer crew of thirty were left, and one still evening after work they were all relaxing in the employees' recreation room, furnished with a broken-down couch and a soft drink machine that was rather arbitrary about keeping the beverages cold or relinquishing them in return for money. This was long before a satellite dish had been installed, and because the area is remote and high in the mountains, no television or radio reception was possible. And since none of the men had record or tape players, they had little to amuse themselves besides conversation.

"We were all talking when suddenly this soft drink machine started making a weird throbbing sound," Rick recalled. "And nobody had anything that would play music, but we heard snatches of a tune that kept coming over the throb of this machine. It was part of Mary

Magdalene's song, 'I Don't Know How to Love Him,' from the musical *Jesus Christ Superstar.*"

Apparently everyone in the room heard the music, which kept fading in and out over the hum of the machine. "The really strange thing was that we weren't hearing just the melody, which would have seemed impossible enough, but the words, too. And it didn't seem to be playing the whole song, but only the refrain, over and over again."

As if that incident were not strange enough, right before sundown, a huge swarm of swallowtail butterflies descended on the men in the recreation room.

"It was one of the last warm days of summer, and they were all around there," Rick said, "flying in and out the windows and around the outside of the building, batting up against the panes of glass. It was very unusual to see so many in one place; it seemed almost idyllic."

The next afternoon, after Rick got in from lunch, he received a telephone call from his parents, informing him that a good friend of his had been killed while mountain climbing near Casper.

"She was very energetic and full of life, the type of person who would try anything once," Rick explained. "She had been taking a climbing class through the college there. Apparently she didn't tie the knots properly or something, and she pitched backwards off a cliff."

The young woman had died just at dusk the evening before, at approximately the same time as the mysterious incidents involving the soft drink machine and the butterflies had occurred.

"Her favorite song was 'I Don't Know How to Love Him,' the one we'd heard playing on the machine, and she really had a thing for butterflies," Rick noted. "I don't know what to make of what happened, except that maybe these things were her way of telling me, 'I'm gone, but death isn't as bad as you think.' She was the kind of person who would do something like that."

GHOSTS
OF THE
FERRIS MANSION

T he Ferris Mansion in Rawlins, Wyoming, is the kind of house that most people can only dream of living in. With its Victorian turret, gingerbread trim, and wide, spacious porches, the 8,000-square-foot, three-story structure at 607 West Maple looks every inch the residence of a prosperous turn-of-the century family. Its present owner, Janice M. Lubbers, admits that she has always had a fondness for old houses, and in her words, "this has got to be the ultimate old house!"

Janice was attracted to the Ferris Mansion ever since she moved to Rawlins during the energy boom of the early 1970s. "I used to sit out front and look at it," she confessed. "And to be able to buy the house in 1979, I had to sell practically everything I owned, but it was worth it. Now I feel that I was meant to live here.

"Before I bought the Ferris Mansion, my daughter Kaye-Marie, her friend Lauren, and I sometimes played with a Ouija board, asking it whether I would be able to purchase the house, and when we would be able to move in. We played with it even after we were living here, and one day when we asked for the name of the spirit controlling the board, we were told that it was someone named Cecil. If we had been consciously or unconsciously moving the planchette ourselves, as some people apparently do when they play with a Ouija, I don't think we would have come up with that name. Kaye-Marie said that she had never heard of it, and I said that I had known only one person named Cecil, a plumber from Minnesota when I was growing up.

"Not long after this, I decided to do some research on the house, especially on the children who had lived here," Janice continued. "Imagine my amazement when I visited the cemetery and saw the name 'Cecil' on a tombstone in the Ferris family plot!

"Seeing the name really piqued my curiosity, so I went to the newspaper offices and started looking through old stories in the morgue. Nine-year-old Cecil Ferris had died in 1904, so that's where I began to search. After I found his obituary, we were frightened to use the Ouija anymore, so we threw it away."

The March 5, 1904, story of the "Awful Accident Which Cost the Life of Little Cecil Ferris" is so sympathetically told and so characteristic of the journalistic treatment of death in the early years of this century that I have excerpted portions as follows:

> A most distressing accident happened Sunday afternoon, shortly after one oclock [sic] which cost a human life.
>
> At that hour Ralph Ferris and his brother Cecil were in a room . . . alone while the other members of the family were busy about the house.
>
> An older brother had brought a pistol home with him and placed it on the table in the bedroom. The young boys got hold of it and in some manner the gun was fired just as Cecil passed through the doorway.
>
> The bullet entered his neck and passed through it, cutting an artery, and Cecil fell to the floor and died instantly.
>
> When the other members of the family reached the room Ralph had the body of his dead brother in his arms. The little fellow was laid on the bed and the doctors summoned, but life had fled and nothing could be done.
>
> The funeral was held from the family residence Tuesday afternoon and was very largely attended.

The Ferris family, originally from Michigan, may have been one of the wealthiest in the West, but their money did not protect them from a series of such tragedies. The father, George Ferris, a member of the territorial legislature in 1877 and of Wyoming's constitutional convention in 1889, earned his fortune from cattle and sheep before becoming the owner of the Ferris-Haggarty copper mine near the town of Encampment, southeast of Rawlins. In 1900, three years before little Cecil's death, sixty-year-old George Ferris had been thrown from his carriage and killed when his team of horses ran away with him on the way home from the mine. His widow, Julia

Childs Ferris, had already lost two of her seven children, and she was to lose not only Cecil, but his older brother Verne in accidents later on.

According to rumors that persist to this day, more tragedy occurred during the construction of the mansion itself. Sometime before the house was completed in 1903, anywhere from one to three workmen were supposedly killed in a fall from the roof, although I have been unable to find anyone either to confirm or deny this report.

Could the many sad things connected with the Ferris family and the house itself be responsible for the psychic phenomena reported by different residents?

Janice and her daughter, Kaye-Marie Lubbers Doebele, have had their share of ghostly manifestations, which began as soon as the family moved in.

"When we bought this place, some people were still living upstairs," Janice explained. "The house had been divided into apartments and had become a cheap place to flop, and part of the agreement was that all the tenants would move out when we moved in. Well, it appeared that one couple wasn't going to be out on time, and I was a little upset about that; but on the first night, I went to bed, anyway, and tried to make the best of the situation. But all night long, I kept hearing the sounds of the tenants stomping around, as if they were trying to make as much noise as possible.

"The next morning I was hopping mad myself, and I decided to go raise hell with those people. But when I went upstairs to complain, I discovered that the tenants had left before we ever moved in!

"In addition to hearing things, we've all experienced the feeling of being watched," Janice said, "and occasionally we've caught glimpses of someone in our peripheral vision."

Daughter Kaye-Marie has seen more than that. "One morning I got up early to go skiing," she remembered, "and as I was getting myself a bowl of cereal in the kitchen, I looked into the parlor to see a woman in a white nightgown watering the plants. At first glance, I thought it was Mother, but then I realized that she wasn't out of bed yet. And even if she were, she wouldn't have been watering plants that early. When I looked again, the woman was gone.

"Another time, I was watching television in a room downstairs when a balloon moved across the floor just as if someone were pulling it along. At first, I thought that air from the furnace might have caused it to travel that way, but then I remembered that we have radiator heat, which produces very few air currents.

"I kept trying to figure out what I had seen as I went to brush my teeth," said Kaye-Marie. "But I had a worse scare in the bathroom when my tube of toothpaste shot off the counter all by itself!"

Janice still remembers how frightened her daughter was. "All of a sudden, she ran screaming out of there and jumped into bed with me," she recalled, "crying and almost hysterical. She swore that the tube of toothpaste moved by itself, that she had never touched it."

Earlier residents Helen Salisbury (who lived in the Ferris Mansion for over thirty years), and Lois Dean (who has another story; see "The Dark Presence") reported nothing of an unusual nature in the house, but the family of Janice Gerstner experienced several strange occurrences.

"We lived in the house not quite a year, just before Janice Lubbers bought it," Janice Gerstner replied. "I used to do a lot of tube painting on cloth, and I always left my supplies out on the dining room table. Often, if I went into another room for a while, when I came back, my paint brushes, scrapers, or little tubes of paint would be missing, only to reappear later.

"I also remember the time that my son was in the bathroom with the door left ajar," she continued. "He started hollering at us to quit walking past the door and to give him some privacy, but no one was even on that side of the house. We were all in the front room. He kept accusing us of lying to him, but we weren't.

"Another unexplained incident occurred while we were there, but I'm not sure that this has anything to do with ghosts," Janice Gerstner added. "For a time I managed the apartments on the property, and no pets were allowed. But one day, when no one was at home, a small, gray, Benji-type of dog somehow appeared on the roof. Nobody had any idea where it came from or whose it was. I was always cleaning the third-floor apartment of some bachelors, so I knew that they weren't hiding any pets up there. But suddenly, here was this dog stranded on the roof, which was so slanted that a workman once told me he would have to use his climbing gear to get onto it. But however the dog got up there, there was no way for it to get down, so someone had to come rescue it."

The mysterious phenomena reported at the Ferris Mansion may extend to the property next door, a house built by Julia Ferris in 1913 for her oldest son, Frank. A story called "The Playroom," included in Margaret Ronan's *The Dynamite Book of Ghosts and Haunted Houses* (New York: Scholastic Book Services, 1980), has long been believed to be about the Ferris Mansion, but Janice Lubbers points to evidence that suggests otherwise.

"The house next door is a smaller version of the Ferris Mansion, and it has been vacant, whereas our house never was. The Ferris Mansion had a barn converted to apartments in the early 1940s, but Frank's house had a carriage house with an apartment above that was original to the place. And the picture on the cover of Ronan's book resembles the cottage next door more than the Ferris Mansion."

Margaret Ronan, who lived in Rawlins when the incident she describes took place, claims in an author's note that all her stories are true, and that some were told to her by the people who experienced them.

"The Playroom" is set in the 1920s, when a lonely little girl named Ethel Shelby had dreams of living in one of the mansions that graced the streets of Rawlins. The twelve-year-old girl used to peer through a wrought-iron fence at her dream house, which was for sale, but which was much too expensive for her family to afford.

Ethel's family had moved to Rawlins two years before, but the shy child had made no friends. Even if she had, she wouldn't have been allowed to bring anyone home, because her brother, Will, was desperately ill with leukemia. One day, Ethel was daydreaming in front of her favorite house when she saw a boy leaning out of the carriage house at the back. He waved at her and told her to come up to visit him.

The boy's name was Roy, and he showed Ethel his playroom in the carriage house. The young girl's eyes sparkled with delight, for here in the big loft were toys of all kinds, including an electric train, books, and games. As elated as Ethel was to have found her new friend, however, she remained puzzled by the circumstances of his life. He said that his family was away, and that he was there in Rawlins only for the summer. And even though the house was for sale and there was not so much as a housekeeper to look after him, Roy said that his needs for meals and clean clothes were "all taken care of."

Ethel spent at least part of every day for the next six weeks with Roy, and she was happier than she had ever been. One day she told her friend about her sick brother and asked whether she could take him one of the toys from the playroom.

"No, not now. I'll save one for him. What would he like?" Roy asked, and Ethel told him that Will would probably like the train the best, if he ever became well enough again to play with it. Or if that was too much, maybe Will could have just one of the cars.

Roy smiled and told her, "I promise you he'll play with the whole train. Did I ever tell you I could see into the future? I see Will up here, playing with the train."

Ethel wondered whether Roy was making fun of her, so she left and promised to come again. But Will died the next day, so Ethel didn't return to the playroom for two weeks. At the end of that time, she remembered that Roy had promised her Will wouldn't die, so she went to tell him how wrong he had been. She took with her the watch that Will had gotten for Christmas, because she wanted Roy to have it.

Ethel passed through the iron gates and heard laughter coming from the carriage house. As she drew closer to the playroom, she heard the electric train chugging along. Roy suddenly appeared at the top of the stairs and demanded to know what she wanted. Ethel told him that she had lots to tell and a present to give.

"I don't need a watch. And I don't need you! I've got a new friend now. Don't come here anymore," Roy said, pushing her toward the stairs and slamming the playroom door, but not quickly enough to prevent Ethel from seeing inside the room.

The young girl ran sobbing all the way home, and when she got there, she grabbed her mother's arm and insisted, "Mama, Will's not dead! He's over at the Wilkerson house. He's playing with Roy's electric train. I saw him!"

Mrs. Shelby stared in disbelief and reminded her daughter that of course Will was dead. Hadn't Ethel been to his funeral? She put her distraught daughter to bed and called the doctor, who gave the girl a shot and claimed that she was acting out of delayed shock and grief.

As Ethel drifted off to sleep, she heard her mother ask, "Who is this Roy? I thought the Wilkerson place was up for sale."

"It is," said the doctor. "There's no one living there at the present. The only Roy I know about was Mr. Wilkerson's younger brother. But he died a long time ago of diphtheria. He was only a kid. There hasn't been a child living in the Wilkerson place since then."

Just as the spirit of little Roy stayed behind in the carriage house, the spirit of Rawlins's early days lives on in the Ferris Mansion, which has now been restored to its original condition and is included in the National Register of Historic Places. "We've taken out all the walls that were added, and we were fortunate that no original walls had been removed," Janice M. Lubbers said. "We have the house back to its original space, and it's a very warm, friendly atmosphere, especially compared to the gloom we faced when we first moved in. The house has sixty-five windows, and we've got lace curtains, so everything is bright and sunny. Nothing unusual has happened recently, and I'm no longer afraid to stay here alone."

The Ferris Mansion, then, seems to be free of ghosts at last. But since Janice has recently turned this lovely house into a bed and breakfast inn, why not come and see for yourself?

THE LIBRARY BUILT
OVER A
CEMETERY

I f you think that ghosts inhabit only old, run-down buildings, think again. The Sweetwater County Library in Green River was opened as recently as 1980, yet it appears to be one of the most haunted spots in Wyoming. And no wonder, when you consider that it was constructed on top of the city's oldest cemetery.

Many of Green River's earliest citizens rested peacefully but anonymously in unmarked graves until 1926. When the grounds were needed for town expansion, however, the bodies were all supposed to be exhumed and moved up the hill to the current cemetery.

Marna Grubb, now the mayor/secretary of Green River, was one of the many curious children who came to watch the gruesome procedure. "Some of the kids on their way to school actually took rings and other things right off the corpses!" she said and shuddered. "I saw only one of the bodies myself, but that was enough. He was just a skeleton, wearing an old western-style, fringed leather jacket. And what was strange was that he still had a red beard."

When housing for veterans was constructed in the area during World War II, it soon became obvious that not all the bodies had been exhumed in 1926. As more remains were discovered, they, too, were reinterred in the new cemetery. After the veterans' residences were no longer needed, the old cemetery grounds were left alone until 1978, when the library purchased them for the site of its new building. As soon as the groundbreaking began, however, workers made yet another grisly discovery: according to architect Neal Stowe of Salt Lake City, from eight to twelve more bodies were found in unmarked graves!

"A heavy Caterpillar was going back and forth, loosening and moving the soil," he explained. "I walked right through the middle of the site, where something that looked like a deteriorated coconut was sitting on top of some freshly churned dirt. I picked the thing up, turned it around, and recognized it as part of a skull. Little tufts of dark brown hair were still clinging to it.

"I stopped the construction immediately and told the contractor that there might be other remains in the area, too. We met with various city representatives to try to determine the extent of the bodies still on the site. Any markings that may have been on the graves had long since been destroyed, and the records of the burials had apparently been misplaced, so it was next to impossible to determine what remains belonged to whom. We walked through the site and started probing with hand shovels, uncovering bits and pieces of wood as well as a variety of decayed bones," the architect said. "The remains were typically buried in old wooden caskets that had deteriorated because of soil conditions."

When the new group of bodies was taken from the site and reburied in a common grave on top of the hill, old bits of hearsay resurfaced. Remembering the Oriental-looking scraps of cloth that had been found in one of the earlier excavations, some people theorized that the cemetery was in fact a Chinese graveyard, even though at least one of the corpses had red hair. Another revived rumor held that the bones were those of smallpox victims and that the town was again endangered by their exposed remains. This conjecture proved as groundless as the other, as a July 12, 1978, article in the *Green River Star* explained. For while Green River's railroad workers had indeed experienced a smallpox epidemic between the 1860s and the 1890s, the victims had all been buried at the far end of the old cemetery and their graves had never been disturbed.

What *was* disturbed, however, was the new library built upon the twice-excavated grounds. Almost from the outset, those who worked there described it as a spooky place, and former maintenance man Ed Johnson* confirms that there are still bodies underneath.

"In the spring of 1983, I helped with the landscaping," he said. "One day the contractors working in front of the main doors dug up a bunch of wood. At first I thought it was old construction debris, but then I saw the bones!

"They called the coroner and started pulling the skeletons out," he recalled. "But then they ran into a problem. Some of the bones were underneath the sidewalk and couldn't be removed without tearing up the concrete. Since the landscapers didn't want to do that, they dug up only parts of those bodies.

"As I remember, first they dug out three adults—actually, I should say two and a half—because on one body they just pulled out the legs and pelvic girdle and left the rest. They also found one infant grave, and I believe they were able to take only the foot and shin bones from it.

"In 1985 and '86, more structural work was necessary, since the building had begun to sink," Ed continued. "While the construction workers were drilling into the foundation, one said that they found a whole, small coffin with the body of another child inside. This corpse was almost perfectly preserved. The flesh was like gelatin, but otherwise, everything was intact."

In spite of these newest ghastly finds under the building, the library employees never lost their sense of humor. "When the construction workers drilled holes in the slab to inject some grout, the staff did one really goofy thing," said library director Helen Higby. "They bought one of those paper skeletons and suspended it so that one arm was sticking out of a hole!"

But the employees were not so amused by the strange actions of the security system one evening in the late summer or early autumn of 1986.

"People leaving the library have to pass through a gate," Helen explained, "and if a book isn't checked out properly, an alarm goes off. There is, however, a bypass which allows people in wheelchairs to leave without going through the gate. The bypass is a little higher than waist level, and it's made of wrought iron. Obviously it can't be too heavy if a wheelchair has to pass through it, but it wouldn't blow in the breeze, either.

"One night two of my staff were the only ones left in the building, and at ten minutes to nine, they were getting ready to close up. Each one was at least fifteen feet away from this bypass, but all of a sudden, it slammed as hard as it could, swung open again, and then oscillated back and forth for several seconds until it came to a stop! It acted as if someone had smashed into it as hard as he could, but nobody was even near it.

"That was the first I'd heard about any unexplained phenomena," Helen continued, "and the two women were so upset that they didn't want to talk about it. But afterwards, I started hearing about other weird things that had happened."

Many of these involved unexplained electrical disturbances. Women staff members on several occasions reported turning off the lights in the multi-purpose room, only to find them on again ten minutes later, with the switch controlling them still in the "off" position. Maintenance men Marlin Dillard and Don Leasor experienced similar disturbances in the same room and on the stairwell, and each time they could determine only that nothing was causing a short.

Ed Johnson was no more successful in finding the cause of mysterious behavior in a vacuum cleaner. "One night after the library had closed, I was running the sweeper back and forth between the book stacks," he said. "Once I moved too far and pulled the plug out of the wall. Naturally, the vacuum quit working, so I turned the switch off and went back down the stacks to plug in the fifty-foot cord. But before I had walked back to turn the switch on again, the vacuum started by itself!"

Ed is positive that the switch was off when the machine came to life. "The next thing I did was to unplug it, wind up the cord, and say to whoever or whatever was there, 'Okay, guys, the building's yours. I'm going home!' Lots of times I'd had feelings that I was being watched, but nothing like this had ever happened before."

Nearly everyone I interviewed reported the same sensation of being watched, especially in the multi-purpose room. A custodian was vacuuming there one day when she happened to glance up at an adjoining stage. The curtains were open, and the stage was set for some upcoming event. The woman thought to herself how nice it looked and went back to her sweeping. When she glanced up again a short while later, the drapes were closed. Because they were operated by an electric opening and closing mechanism, the woman reasoned that one of the control switches must be at the circulation desk, and that the staff there were playing tricks on her. Upon confronting them, however, she discovered that the only switch for the curtains was the one in the multi-purpose room itself.

Maintenance man Don Leasor had another eerie experience while vacuuming, when he heard what sounded like someone "rattling the heck out of a keychain."

"Whatever was making the noise was in the same room with me," he explained. "And whenever I'd shut the vacuum off, the noise would stop, too."

Don has probably experienced more unnerving incidents than anyone else. Several times since he began working in April 1986, he has seen mysterious glowing lights inside the building.

"The first time," he said, "I was getting ready to walk out the door, so I turned off the lights in the front room. About five seconds later, I saw small glowing lights moving over the wall, right above the entry way, just as if someone were shining little flashlights with eight-inch diameters of illumination. The glowing would appear and disappear every three or four seconds."

Don is certain that he was not seeing reflections from passing automobiles. "I've seen car lights shining from the street and into the library, but these looked nothing like that."

Even more upsetting was the experience shared by Don and former custodian Marlin Dillard. "We were upstairs, in a different part of the library, but we could hear distinctly what sounded like somebody latching the doors to the multi-purpose room," said Marlin. "Then, when we went down to look, nobody else was anywhere in the building." Strangest of all was the fact that the doors were not even pulled shut when the two men came to inspect them!

Another time Don heard strains of "something that sounded like Beethoven" coming from the piano in this same multi-purpose room. "I heard just a little of it, but then it stopped. And there was absolutely no one else around," he said. "What made this even creepier was that it happened the same night that the gate swung back and forth by itself."

Perhaps his scariest experience was hearing voices, however. "One night when I was carrying out the trash, I thought I heard people talking," he said. "So I set the trash outside and closed the door as if I'd already left. Apparently, whatever was in the building thought I had. But then I sneaked back inside and heard the voices coming from the multi-purpose room. It sounded like a man and a woman yelling and arguing, although the words were muffled so I couldn't tell what they were saying. And since I had just come through that part of the library before taking out the trash, I knew no one was there.

"I even checked to make sure that the noise wasn't coming from outdoors," Don said. "But finally, I gathered up my nerve and opened the door to that room. As soon as I did, the voices immediately stopped!"

Don Leasor was not the only staff member to hear the strange voices. A former maintenance assistant who was too terrified to be interviewed claimed that she often heard them when she worked alone from eight until ten at night.

Since so many frightening things were taking place late in the evening, library director Helen Higby rearranged schedules and made it a rule that no one worked alone.

"Even if it turns out that there's nothing there," she pointed out, "if someone were to get nervous and imagine something, then trip and fall down the stairs, we might not find them until the next day. And we've got enough ghosts already!"

Not long after the new policy took effect, the business manager came in to do some work on a holiday, and mindful of the new rule, she brought her Doberman pinscher along. "After she had been in her office for a while," Helen said, "the dog suddenly went over to the door and cocked its head as if someone were outside. Then it came back and sat down in the middle of the room, but it continued to stare at the door, fully alert. That's all that happened, but it gave everybody the creeps, because dogs, unlike people, don't imagine things.

"At one of the staff meetings," Helen continued, "I told everyone, 'Listen, I know how to deal with budget cuts; I know how to deal with all kinds of normal problems. But I don't know how to deal with spooks!' So we talked about the possibility of getting an exorcist, about having a priest come and bless the building, but some of the employees didn't want that. In their minds, that gave credence to something they didn't want to think about."

Apparently nothing out of the ordinary had been reported for a year or so at the time of my interviews in February 1988, but it is unknown whether the phenomena have stopped or are just not as noticeable now that workers are forbidden to be alone in the building. Skeptics might conclude that the new rule provides less opportunity for overactive imaginations to concoct spooky stories, but with so much evidence from so many people, it seems clear that something of an unusual nature was occurring. Even former librarian Grace Gasson, who attributes the disturbances to the building's structural defects and the susceptible imaginations of the living, admits that she has no explanation for such things as the wildly oscillating security gate.

If the troublesome manifestations at the Sweetwater County Library were indeed of a paranormal nature, what caused them? Do the spirits of the dead really return to wreak havoc when their resting place is disturbed? No one I interviewed believed that the spirits were of a malicious nature. As Helen Higby observed, "Whatever is going on, if it's some kind of being, apparently it's benign, because it hasn't done anything destructive or harmful. And in a library, you could make a big mess in a hurry if you wanted to, by throwing the books on the floor or dumping the card catalogues."

Whatever caused the strange events at the library, most of the staff are less inclined to scoff at the supernatural these days. And even without the new rule, the odds are that you'd have a hard time finding anyone willing to spend the night there alone!

THE GHOST
IN THE
RED FLANNEL SHIRT

n 1951, seventeen-year-old Phil Johnson* was hunting elk with his father and a group of other men in Wyoming's majestic Bighorn Mountains. On a cold, cloudy dawn their party left camp to hunt in the timber of North Trapper Creek. They were lucky to run into a herd of elk by midmorning, and each hunter was successful in bringing down his prey. For the rest of the morning and into the early afternoon, the men cleaned and tagged their game. Then they rested and talked, enjoying the outdoors and each other's company.

As midafternoon rolled around, the weather turned colder and a heavy fog began to settle in. Phil was the youngest in the hunting party, so he was elected to walk back to camp to get the pickup truck and bring it to where the men and their quarry were waiting.

Because Phil knew the area so well, his father was not worried that he would lose his way back to the camp, which was two to three miles distant, across two canyons and North Trapper Creek. But before Phil had gone very far, the fog got heavier. As the white mist rolled in all around him, almost completely obscuring his view, he lost his bearings and couldn't tell whether he had crossed one or both of the small canyons. But he plunged ahead, and the farther he walked, the steeper and rougher the terrain became.

"I knew then that things weren't right," Phil said. "The fog by that time was so thick that I couldn't make out any familiar landmarks. I considered staying put, building a large fire, and waiting it out, the way I had been taught. But for some reason I kept going. I was getting very tired and a little panicky when I suddenly looked up into a clearing.

"There was a faint image of a young boy standing there. He was wearing a red flannel shirt and pointing in the direction opposite to where I was headed. I hollered at him, but before he could say or do anything else, the fog moved into the clearing and he disappeared.

"Still not knowing where I was, I began walking in the direction he had pointed, and I soon came to a road. I followed it and walked right into our camp.

"I waited until the fog lifted; then I drove the pickup to where my dad and the rest of the hunters were waiting. I asked if anyone had seen a young kid with a red flannel shirt, but everyone said no. We loaded up the game and drove back to camp.

"When it was dark, we hung up our elk in the trees. I kept thinking about what I had seen, knowing somehow that it hadn't been a real person standing there. I was still bothered about it the next day, so I left our group and drove over to a nearby hunting camp to ask if any of their party had gotten lost in the fog.

"One of the men said he had. He had begun to lose his sense of direction when suddenly he saw a boy in a red flannel shirt, who motioned urgently for him to stay where he was. Taking heed, the man built a fire on a ridge and stayed there all night. When he started back to camp the next morning, he discovered that if he had kept moving in the thick fog, he would have walked right off a very steep ledge.

"He told me that there had been something strange about that boy, and as tired as he was from the day's ordeal, he hadn't been able to sleep. I didn't tell him that I had stayed awake the night before for the same reason."

Nor did Phil recount his tale to the old Basque sheep herder in Greybull, who told the astonished young man that only the year before, he had encountered the apparition of a boy who got lost and died on Trapper Creek. In the past, Phil would have regarded such a story as a tall tale to be told around campfires, but now he knew better.

"Being as young and scared as I was, however, I just kept this story bottled up inside me for more than thirty-five years, until now,"

—

he said. "I've been hunting and fishing in the Trapper Creek area many times since 1951, but I've never seen any more apparitions, and I don't know if anyone besides the elk hunter or the sheep herder has, either."

Did the spirit of the young boy lost on Trapper Creek really return to spare others from his own fate? Or were those who saw him so tired, frightened, and confused that they simply hallucinated the image of a boy giving directions that, merely by coincidence, turned out to be right? Regardless of the answers to these questions, it is undeniable that at least two men may owe their very lives to that figure in the red flannel shirt.

HOW TO
REFORM A
HAUNTED HOUSE

I t's very rare in the history of haunted houses for a dilapidated, sinister abode to be transformed into a bright, cheerful family dwelling, especially if it retains its otherworldly occupants in spite of the change! But that apparently is what has happened to the home of Leigh and Virgil Wilson and their two children, Angye and Shain Wacaster.

When the family took up residence in June 1984, the 1890s-era house in Sheridan, Wyoming, could have served as the backdrop for any of Bela Lugosi's movies. "The first thing my daughter said was 'Oh, my God, Mom, you don't want to live here!'" Leigh said in her charming southern drawl. "And my husband told me, 'You're crazy! I'm not moving into *that*! Do you know how much it would cost to remodel it?'

"It *was* creepy," Leigh admitted, "with dark paneling and ugly green carpeting, and much of the interior painted black. But we needed a place to live, and the purchase price was cheap, so we bought it."

It wasn't long before they realized that their new residence came with spooks included. Leigh was lying in bed one night when she felt someone brush the hair from her face. "I sprang up from the pillow and told Virgil that an intruder was in the room," she said. "He told me to go back to sleep, that it was probably just a moth, or maybe even a mouse. But that didn't help—I was more scared of the mouse than I would have been of a ghost!

"Not much later Virgil himself had a run-in with the phantom. He had been about to use the telephone when some invisible person laid a hand on his shoulder. This particular ghost must be very attracted to him, because one night when Virgil was sitting in his chair watching television, he felt someone behind him stroking his hair. At first he thought I was doing it, but when he turned around to look, he saw that no one was even in the same room with him. Another time, in the bedroom, he felt someone softly touching his face."

This demonstrative spirit is not always gentle, however, as Leigh found out one night when she and her children were watching TV in the living room. "All of a sudden, I felt a hand grab my knee, and an electrical shock ran down my leg," she said. "I was frightened and yelled, and my son ran over and pulled a piece of wire out of my knee! The wound never bled, but Shain was so scared that he came and sat beside me for the rest of the evening.

"All of us have sensed a presence in the house," Leigh continued, "and when we first moved in, I always felt that someone was in the bathroom with me. One night I was just about to step into the shower when I distinctly heard the floor squeak as someone got in ahead of me! 'Look,' I told whoever it was, 'you can go anywhere in this house that you want to, but you're not taking a shower with me!'

"No one bothers me anywhere now, but there used to be a terribly oppressive feeling in Shain's room," Leigh went on. "I always felt that something didn't want me in there. A couple of times as I walked down the hall, the door to his room would be open, but I couldn't force myself to go inside. I don't know why, but I always felt that if I went through that door, I wouldn't come out again.

"Our dogs, all Siberian huskies, have been sensitive to presences, too. In our living room where we've got a woodstove, there used to be a window, but it was boarded up before we came," Leigh said. "One of my dogs and I were sitting on the sofa watching TV one day, and she kept looking toward where the window had been and wagging her tail. Then she started acting as if someone were behind me, so I moved to a different part of the room!

"Another time, I felt a little scared, so I brought one of our other dogs into the house to keep me company. She was lying by my feet, but she left repeatedly to look up the stairs.

114

"I don't know what the dogs saw, but I've seen several apparitions myself," Leigh insisted. "I saw the first one when I was painting my son's room. All the furniture had been moved out, and I was up on a ladder, painting the ceiling, when I happened to glance down and catch a glimpse of a woman with her arms folded, sitting in a rocking chair and watching me paint. At first I didn't believe what I saw, so I looked again, but she was still there. I wish I had had the presence of mind to question her, but the only thing I could think to say was 'I'm doing the best I can!' And then she disappeared!

"She looked to be between fifty and fifty-five years old, with dark hair pulled back into a bun. She wore a dark dress with an apron that went around the neck, and she looked completely solid. She'd even brought along her own rocking chair, because there was nothing in that room but me and the ladder and the paint. If I were to see a picture of her, I would still recognize her, even though I've seen her only once.

"Three times, however, I saw a younger lady dressed in white. I would be standing at the kitchen sink washing dishes or doing some other chore when I sensed someone behind me. When I turned to look, I would see her passing through the kitchen door and into the dining room, where she always disappeared. I could see only part of her, from the middle of her hips on up, and she looked misty. As she walked through the door, she would turn and look at me, but I wasn't scared of her. She looked pretty and young, probably in her twenties, with very long brown hair, and she wore what might have been a white nightgown. When we remodeled the kitchen, we put the door opening in a different place and plastered over where it had been. I haven't seen her since, and I kind of miss her."

Leigh is familiar with the theory that remodeling buildings can first cause, then later terminate supernatural phenomena, and she agreed that the manifestations became fewer as more reconstruction was done. The idea behind this theory is that many ghostly sights, sounds, and even odors, are nothing more than psychic impressions recorded on their surroundings, which may "play back" the data if conditions are favorable. Therefore, by exposing long-covered walls and floorboards, for example, one might very well create the conditions necessary for certain recorded information to be duplicated, just as one hears music when a tape recorder is switched on. By the same token, altering the structures may destroy the impressions or their ability to be played back. This theory also helps explain why sometimes only part of a ghost is seen, as in the case of the legless lady in white. Only a portion of the recorded impressions might have survived, and of those survivors, only a portion might meet the conditions necessary to be reproduced.

Another "partial" ghost was also witnessed in the living room, when Leigh saw an odd assortment of limbs rising from her sofa. "I saw a man's right leg from the thigh to the foot, and his right arm, and he seemed to be pushing his hand against the cushion to hoist himself up after lying down," she explained. "He was whitish pink, and the hand that I saw was big. He had no shoes or pants that I could see, and no dark hair on his body."

Virgil suggested that the apparition might have had something to do with his father, who died on the sofa in his own home in Michigan. "But if that's true, I'm not certain why he would appear to me as he did in Wyoming," Leigh said.

Another phantom, a dog, trotted through the open front door one summer day while Leigh was working in the living room. "You could see right through it," she recalled. "It was a little slick-haired, white terrier with black markings, who disappeared as soon as it walked in the door.

"My eeriest encounter, though, took place one night after work. I was employed at a restaurant, and it was my job to close, so I'd get home at one or two o'clock in the morning. My family always left some lights on for me, and as I unlocked the door, I saw someone's shadow in the kitchen. I thought it was Virgil, so I walked all through the downstairs, hollering for him, but he wasn't there. When I walked up to the top of the stairs, I saw a smaller shadow duck into my son's room, so I assumed that it was Shain. He was sound asleep, however.

"I went into the bathroom and started getting undressed, when I saw a white cloud, about two feet from the floor, whirling as fast as it could go. I was so panic-stricken that I ran into our room, jumped in bed, and told Virgil what I had seen. " 'That's nothing!' he said. 'This bed has been shaking ever since I got into it tonight!'

"We were troubled by shaking beds almost from the moment we moved in here," Leigh declared. "But since we live only about a block and a half from the railroad tracks, we reasoned that the vibrations were causing the jiggling. When it happened over and over again, however, we realized that the beds shook even when no trains were passing through.

"It was as if somebody were under the bed pushing up with his feet, because we could see and feel the mattress moving up and down. Other times, it felt as if someone were at the foot of the bed, pushing his hands down to make a big jolt. One night when I was trying to read, I finally had had enough, so I said, 'Okay, if you've got something to tell me, you sit down and do it. If you don't, get out right now!' And the shaking quit."

Leigh's son Shain also suffered from a "nervous" bed. "Lots of times, I felt someone sitting on it," he explained. "I'd be lying there, and I could see and feel the bed sag down in one spot. After a while, I could feel whoever it was getting up.

"A few years ago, I was listening to some heavy metal music, some Satanic stuff, before going to sleep," he remembered. "My bed suddenly jumped a few inches off the floor and almost knocked me out of it before it started back down. The second it began to move, I turned off the music, because I had the feeling that somebody didn't want me listening to it. For some reason, I don't listen to that kind of music much anymore!"

Virgil had the scariest bedtime story of all, however, when he felt something "with the nastiest smell he had ever smelled" actually crawl into bed with him.

Leigh attributes the worst of these physical manifestations to a period of heightened family tensions a few years ago. During that time, a diamond-shaped black and white mirror in Shain's room crashed to the ground for no good reason. "It had been hanging behind his chest of drawers, on which he kept an assortment of bottles and other things," Leigh explained. "Against that same wall were a bookcase and a table; and I don't know how the mirror did it, but the only way it could have fallen was to slide to the left all the way across the wall and then down. Because nothing was knocked over, broken, or disturbed in any way, except for the mirror itself, which shattered into a million pieces.

"Another time, when I was in the bathroom, the shower suddenly turned itself on and sprayed full force, but only for a second. And during an especially stressful time, I was alone in the bedroom when the door began moving in an in-and-out fashion as if it were breathing. At first I thought the wind was blowing it, since the windows in my daughter Angye's room were open, but when I got up to check, I saw that there was absolutely no breeze."

Much worse was the time a religious ornament suddenly transformed itself before her and Virgil's eyes. "The house was so spooky at first that I made a ceramic crucifix," explained Leigh, "and Virgil put it up in the hallway next to our bedroom door. I was walking up the stairs one day and he was behind me, when I began to stare at the crucifix. 'Can ceramics melt? Look at that!' I said, and if Virgil hadn't seen it, too, I would have doubted my own eyes. On one side, the face of Jesus Christ appeared to have melted. We went closer to examine it, and as we stood watching, it suddenly reverted to its former appearance!"

Along with the physical manifestations are the unexplained sounds that the family often hears, at all times of the day or night. "Months will go by without our hearing anything, and then everything starts happening!" Leigh said. "We've heard boxes tumbling around upstairs, but when we go to look, everything's in place. One night Virgil and I both heard the footsteps of little kids running down the hallway. We could tell by the number of steps they took that whoever was making the sound wasn't very big, but we checked on both our teenagers, anyway, and found them asleep. Sometimes we hear knocking on our bedroom door when no one is outside it, and my son says that he often hears me calling his name when I'm not there. And one night when I was lying in bed, I could have sworn that my daughter was right beside me, saying 'Mom, Mom.' But when I looked up, no one was there.

"A very strange thing occurred about eight o'clock one morning," Leigh continued. "I was alone in the house, having a cup of coffee, and looking right at the front door. I suddenly heard people walk down the stairs and open and shut the door, but I could see that it never moved an inch. I guess it was just some ghosts going off to work!

"Virgil and I have also heard what sounds like the rustling of old-fashioned clothing in our bedroom. There used to be a woodstove in one spot, and the rustling always seems to be heading toward it.

"But the most disconcerting sound is that of a man laughing or coughing. I've heard him only once, when I was in bed reading. His laughter was faint and sounded something like an echo, as if he were far away. One night when Shain was on the telephone, he heard the man cough, and then he felt him sit down on his bed.

"The most persistent manifestations seem to be the smells, however," Leigh said. "All of us have smelled both good and bad odors for which there are no explanations, but strangely enough, no two family members have ever smelled anything at the same time. The unpleasant smells are putrid, like decaying flesh, but the nice ones remind us of lilacs, apples, or roses, except that they're so strong they can be sickening. It's as if someone were standing right next to you drenched in perfume, but the scent is neither mine nor my daughter's."

Why have so many incidents of a mysterious nature taken place at this house, one of the oldest in Sheridan? When Leigh checked courthouse records, she found no clues to the various hauntings. It is tempting, therefore, to wonder whether one of Shain's dreams offers an explanation.

"There's an old piano rotten with age that sits outside in the yard," he said. "I looked inside it once and saw that it was made in 1876, and my dream was set in the period when it would have been in the house. I dreamed that a ball was being held here. All the men were in tuxedos, and all the ladies were in wedding dresses. Some of the people were just sitting or walking or dancing, but a lot of them were flying through the air, going up the stairs or through the hallway. And I saw one of the men grab a woman and throw her off the balcony."

An odd coincidence is that at approximately the same time Shain had the dream, around 2 A.M., Virgil woke up to the sound of a woman screaming in terror.

"We wonder if the two incidents could be related," Leigh said. "I wonder, too, whether the lady in white that I saw could have been the one he dreamed about. I don't think she was wearing a wedding dress when I saw her, but it was definitely something white."

If Shain's dream doesn't explain the haunting, another theory is that the family brought their ghosts with them. "This isn't the first time that strange things have happened in a house we've lived in," Leigh confessed. "In Kentucky, we were in a house that was almost brand new, but no one before or after us ever stayed in it longer than six months. Strange things occurred in the next place we moved, too. That house was really evil, and others before us had had trouble there. I know if we had stayed in it any longer, we probably never would have gotten out. So when we moved from Kentucky, I wondered if these things could follow us."

Regardless of the reasons for the haunting, the number of incidents continues to decrease as the house is restored. The formerly black interiors have been painted white, and Leigh says that the atmosphere has changed from gloomy and oppressive to light and happy.

"It still *looks* like a haunted house on the outside," she admitted with a laugh, "but now it feels like a friendly place on the inside. Our family's attitudes have changed, too, and we don't allow any more negative thinking. I used to be frightened to be alone in the house, but I actually feel protected here now. Once during the remodeling, for example, I fell through·some boards upstairs and almost landed in the den below. But I felt something holding me up, keeping me from going all the way down.

"And just the other day when we had built a fire in the stove, the smoke alarm went off. The air was perfectly smoke-free, but I checked the stove, anyway, and found that it was getting dangerously hot. I thanked whoever had sent the warning, because without it, the chimney might have caught fire.

"So we still have unexplained phenomena, especially the smells," Leigh said. "But we've come to look upon them as indications of what is about to happen. When we detect the odor of decay, for example, we know that something bad is about to take place; whereas if we smell the sweet scents, we know that something good is headed our way. We're not afraid of anything in the house anymore—if there are still spirits here, they're friendly and helpful."

If there's a moral to Leigh Wilson's story, then, it must be that mutual respect and cooperation are essential to the harmony and smooth running of any household—*especially* when some of its members happen to be ghosts!

THE HAUNTED AUDITORIUM

omething about a stage is irresistible to ghosts. Theaters all over the earth abound with tales of hauntings by spectral players and patrons, who continue to find the world of make-believe just as compelling as they did in life.

Who, then, haunts the auditorium at Northwest College in Powell? Assistant professor of theater Kermit Herd recalled the first time that anything spooky happened there. "It was in the early 1970s, when we were rehearsing *The Miracle Worker*," he said. "A fellow who had studied parapsychology was on the stage, holding his hands a few inches apart and saying, 'Come tell me if you feel anything within this space.' I know this sounds crazy, but when I put my hand where he indicated, it was like plunging it into ice water. Some of the cast members repeated the experiment, and they all reported the same sensation of extreme cold.

"From then on," Kermit said, "lots of weird things have happened in the auditorium. More than once when I've been in the audience watching the performers, the stage lights have gone haywire. They've gone out, and they've gone down; and one guy who was a real skeptic used to run up to the dimmer board, sure that somebody was playing a joke on us. But no one was ever at the controls.

"And there's a front-row seat, the third from the left in the middle aisle, that is often found in the down position, just as if someone invisible were sitting on it. This usually happens right before a play opens. The chairs are spring-loaded, so that when people rise from them, the seats are supposed to pop back up. Many times we have moved that seat to its upright position when we left for the evening, only to find it down again the next morning.

"One of the oddest incidents took place during a dress rehearsal," Kermit continued. "I was sitting in the audience, watching the actors work through a scene. We had put an antique rocking chair on one of the side stages, and I suddenly heard this creak, creak, creak. At first I was angry that somebody was making noise while we were rehearsing, but when I looked over at the chair, I saw that it was rocking by itself!

"A few days later, during the third performance of the play, one of the actors placed a white shawl on top of the same chair. I was watching from the audience again when the rocker started to move, and this time it rocked so hard that it knocked the shawl right off onto the floor! I don't think that vibrations from the stage caused that to happen, though, because the hardwood floor absorbs a lot of motion," Kermit explained. "And later, when some of the kids *tried* to make the chair rock by jumping up and down, they couldn't get it to move at all.

"It was around this same time that a drama student was alone in the green room, writing risque limericks on the chalk board to amuse himself. Suddenly he got the feeling that somebody was watching him, and when he glanced over his shoulder, the chalk still in his hand, he saw a woman standing there! She didn't say a word, but she smiled at him, so maybe she thought his limericks were funny!" Kermit said and laughed. "She was a perfectly friendly ghost, but he was so startled that he inadvertently broke the chalk against the board and left a big white streak that went straight up from where he'd left off writing! He wouldn't go back into that room for a long time after that.

"He described the apparition as a woman about five feet, four inches tall, with shoulder-length blonde hair that was beginning to turn gray. She was wearing an old-fashioned dress, not like pioneer women wore, but more like those worn by Eastern European folk dancers, with different colors of embroidery on the top. I don't know why, but some of the kids started calling her Adelaide; and from then on, they blamed all the strange occurrences on her. Nobody had any idea who she was or why she was there," said Kermit. "I think she just liked to watch the plays."

While the ghost called Adelaide seemed harmless enough, the same cannot be said of a menacing presence that Kermit himself experienced. "One time I was doing some work on the stage, and when I turned the lights on, I saw something clear in the back on the left side of the auditorium. It was dark and had very little shape, almost like a black cloud, and I sensed that it was pure evil. I don't frighten easily, but that time I was so terrified that the hair on the back of my neck stood up! I left the stage in a hurry and went back to the makeup room, telling myself that I was being stupid and was just imagining things. But three times I went back in to find the thing still there, and the feeling was so intense that I couldn't remain on the stage.

"Finally, the fourth time, I decided to confront whatever it was. I have a very evil-sounding stage laugh, so I stood there on the stage and hollered and dared the thing to do something; then I just started laughing at it, and pretty soon the oppressive feeling went away, along with the black cloud.

"At that time, my office was in the makeup room, and I was the only one who had a key to it. After I confronted the thing in the auditorium, I locked my office door and went home around midnight. The next morning the door was still locked, but the room had been ransacked. All of my books and everything from the shelves and the desk had been thrown to the floor. A couple of vases and some other breakable things had been smashed, and everything had been pulled out of the desk drawers and strewn all over. I never found out who did it, but I'd guess that it was either a very angry spirit or some student who didn't like me very much!"

Duane Fish was one of Kermit's students and is now an associate professor of speech communications at Northwest. He remembers an unexplained occurrence from his own college days in the early 1970s, during the performance of the play based upon the Book of Job, *J.B.* by Archibald Macleish.

"We had placed two tables off to stage left. One that was used in another scene had several place settings on it, including cups, glasses, and plates. The other table held the props, including the masks of God and Satan and some rags that became Job's clothing when he was destitute. The play itself is highly emotional, and right in the climax of the scene where God and Satan confront each other, a cold, rushing wind blew down from the overhead catwalk and knocked all the stuff off of the prop table, as well as the cups on the other one. It was perfect timing, but none of us could figure out where it came from, because the stage is certainly not drafty, especially back in the corner where the tables were. And the wind didn't come from the stage itself, but from somewhere up above. It was a very cold breeze for a while, but then the air became calm again."

Could the same mysterious force have been responsible for an occurrence about ten years ago? According to Eric Lampman's article from Halloween 1985 in the college newspaper, *The Northwest Trail,* some students from previous years had just finished designing the set for a play. Several trees had been nailed securely to the floor with heavy-duty nails, and the lights were dimmed to show what the set looked like in the dark. Before the lights came back on, however, one of the trees appeared to lift straight into the air before crashing to the floor. The set makers immediately examined the tree and discovered that the nails were still embedded in it. Apparently something had just jerked it out of the stage floor, then cast it down again.

From time to time, a new story circulates about the ghost in the auditorium at Northwest College, but no one has come any nearer to understanding the phenomena that have occurred there. For now, all that seems certain is that someone still carefully watches what goes on.

THE PREMONITION
OF
DEATH

O ne night a few years ago, Terry Calkins was returning
to Cody on the Meeteetse highway after an exhausting
day in the oil field. He was looking forward to relaxing
at home and forgetting about work for the evening when
his attention was suddenly drawn to a diesel truck by the side of
the road. On its flatbed he caught a glimpse of the wrecked remains
of a very unusual white pickup with a purple stripe down its side.
From the way the truck was crumpled and smashed, it appeared
to have rolled for quite a distance.

"I've lived here all my life, and I make a point of noticing practically
all the outfits around," explained Terry. "But I had never seen a white
one with a purple stripe like that, other than the one that belonged
to my friend Bruce."

Naturally, Terry was alarmed by what he had seen, and as soon
as he got home, he asked his wife if she had heard anything about
Bruce's being in an accident.

"She said no, so I started calling around and asking people who
knew him if he had wrecked his truck. But nobody knew what I
was talking about."

125

Only a few hours later, Terry found out that his friend had indeed been in an accident, and that his injuries were fatal. He had apparently misnegotiated a corner and plunged off a hill; then the truck had rolled a long way before coming to a stop.

"But his accident happened about two hours *after* I saw what I did," Terry insisted. "I've thought about this for a long time, and sometimes I'm not even sure that I really did see a wrecked truck. At the time, I couldn't figure out why a diesel would be carrying it. I wonder if I just caught a glimpse of a truck on a flatbed and had some kind of hallucination that it was Bruce's. But I would have picked it out in a second as his, because it was so distinctive.

"When I heard that he died, I got a terrible, weird feeling right in my gut. Whatever I saw was definitely a premonition of his death."

A CASE OF
PSYCHIC SENSITIVITY?

P arapsychologists don't know why, but some people seem more sensitive than others to the presence of psychic phenomena. True, some people are more willing than others to give credence to things they don't understand, but beyond that, the reasons for one person's ability to see a ghost or to display telekinetic powers and another's apparent inability to do so are still unclear.

Jo Ann Heimer of Powell is one of the lucky ones (or unlucky, depending upon your point of view) who is evidently receptive to a wide range of psychic phenomena. As is often the case, she first became aware of this receptivity during adolescence.

"One night in the late 1960s, when I was in junior high school, I suddenly woke up with the feeling that someone was watching me," she said. "Still drowsy, I turned around to face the door of my bedroom, where I saw two men walking out. I wasn't really awake enough to have it dawn on me what I was seeing, but I do remember thinking that it was strange; then I rolled over to go back to sleep.

"The next morning at breakfast, I was still thinking about what had happened, and I asked my dad if he had been in my room. When he said he hadn't, I explained that I had seen the two men, and I described them as completely as I could. One had been shorter than the other, and one had been wearing a floppy hat. As they left the room, they looked as though they had been talking to each other. They glanced back into my room, then went through the door. I didn't recognize them.

"After I talked with my parents, we came to the conclusion that the men might have been my two deceased grandfathers who had come to visit me for some reason," Jo Ann continued. "My dad said that his father, whom I had never seen, often wore a floppy hat like the one I had described. I never saw them, or any other phantoms, again."

Because of the circumstances of the sighting, it is possible that what Jo Ann saw was not two ghosts, but images resulting from a fairly common phenomenon. Paranormal investigator and writer Guy Lyon Playfair explains it in *The Haunted Pub Guide:*

> It is well known that many people have the ability to see what are called hypnagogic images when they are in the drowsy state immediately preceding sleep, or when they are in the "hypnopompic" state between sleep and full wakefulness. ... Apparitions are frequently sighted in bedrooms, when the brain of the witness is likely to be in the relaxed state you seem to need if you want to see either a hypnagogic image or a ghost (London: Harrap Limited, 1985, 38).

Yet if the images Jo Ann saw were produced in this way by her own mind, it is unclear why she would have given one of the men a floppy hat. She was apparently unaware that her paternal grandfather was accustomed to wearing one; also, at the time of the sighting, she obviously had no idea as to the identity of her "bedroom invaders."

Other odd occurrences, this time of the poltergeist variety, also took place during her teen years. "One day I had taken a shower and needed to dry off," Jo Ann remembered. "The towels were all stacked in a bin that goes way back into the wall. I had just gotten one and was starting to dry myself, when suddenly about six or eight of them started flying out at me! They came popping right out, one after the other, and landed on the cabinet and the bathroom floor. I wondered what in the world was happening, because it wasn't as if the towels had been on the edge of the bin and were about to fall out—they had been neatly stacked. And anyway, if they had fallen, they wouldn't have come darting out one at a time.

"Another day when I was home by myself, I was vacuuming in the living room when one of the lamps suddenly came on. Naturally, I had to ask myself whether I had turned it on and then forgotten about it. But I was almost positive that I hadn't, because I had been busy vacuuming and then just noticed that the light was on.

"Someone once explained to me that my going through puberty might have caused these things to happen, that some adolescents, especially girls, have this unconscious, uncontrolled telekinetic energy that results in poltergeist activity. I don't know if that's true or not, but I know I wasn't aware of doing these things on purpose."

Whether or not the teenaged Jo Ann possessed unconscious powers of kinesis is uncertain, but it now appears possible that both she and her mother possess some degree of consciously directed telekinetic energy, as evidenced by their experiment with an Excedrin bottle. "We stuck a pin in the top of the bottle and then put a paper on top of the pin," Jo Ann recalled. "We wanted to see if by holding hands and concentrating with all our might, we could turn the paper around. But instead of the paper moving, the whole bottle turned slightly! Neither one of us said anything at first, because we thought we were seeing things. But finally my mother broke the silence to ask if I, too, had seen the bottle move. After that, we quit the experiment, because the results were too spooky!"

A favorite pastime called "Up Table, Rise Table" has also demonstrated their telekinetic powers. In this game, the players hold their hands over the top of a card table, lightly touching it. By concentrating, they are supposed to be able to make the table tilt on two legs at a time, and then, if the energy present is strong enough, to cause the entire table to rise off the floor. One time, Jo Ann, her mother, and a neighbor girl were playing the game, and Jo Ann's brother Danny was making fun of them.

"He was standing in the doorway to his room, making all kinds of remarks about how he didn't believe in what we were doing," Mrs. Heimer remembered. "And suddenly that table just vibrated! Almost as if it were angry. I know it sounds silly, but it began to shake."

"The table then tilted toward me," Jo Ann said, "and someone said, 'Okay, Table, go get Danny!' I was the only one still touching it at this time, and it started tilting and rocking all the way through the dining room until it pinned him in a corner! I was touching the table top the whole time, but I wasn't making the table move. There's no way you can manipulate it that way with your hands just resting on the top. Danny was scared, so I decided that was enough, and took my hands off of it.

"Another time," Jo Ann continued, "we were playing the same game, and my dad brought a glass of water into the room. He was standing there drinking it, and we were talking about the fact that he didn't believe we could levitate the table. He said, 'Yeah, I don't believe in any of this,' and he set the glass on it. Then he said,

'Okay, Table, if you're real, spill this glass of water.' And that table tilted just enough that we could see it was going to spill the water, so we made it stop before the floor actually got wet!"

Other mysterious events were not so easy to blame on psychic energy running amok, so another type of haunting may also be present. "All of us in the family have heard our back door open and close when nobody's there," Jo Ann said. "We'll hear the door open, and we'll expect whoever it is to walk on into the house, but after a minute or so has passed, no one does."

Jo Ann's mother recounted a time when she had been out shopping. "I came home with my groceries," she said, "and my husband met me at the door. He said, 'Good grief! Where were you? I thought I heard you come into the kitchen about an hour ago and set those groceries down, but you weren't anywhere around!'"

The most recent unexplained occurrence in the house took place in the autumn of 1988. "I was sleeping very soundly about midnight or one o'clock in the morning, when all of a sudden, I was awakened by something that grabbed my head and shook it from side to side," Mrs. Heimer explained. "It felt like somebody grabbed me by the mouth, with fingers on one side and the thumb on the other, pinching my face and forcing my head to move against my will. At first I thought my husband had done it, and I was ready to do battle! But when I was able to look over at him, he was asleep. So then I sat up on the side of the bed, not really frightened, but puzzled. It couldn't have been just a dream, because I could still feel the pinching pressure of those fingers and that thumb for a long time afterwards. And I don't see how I could have done it to myself in my sleep, because when I woke up, my hands weren't anywhere near my face. After a while, I got up and walked through the house just to make sure that my husband and I were alone. This was the strangest experience I have ever had!"

Nothing in the history of the house in the northeast part of Powell can explain the weird goings on there. The Heimers built it themselves, and they have been the only ones to live in it.

"Years ago, a Ouija board told us that we had a ghost, and that his name was Barney," Jo Ann said. "So he's the one we've always blamed for all the odd things that have taken place, including the ones that happened to me when I was a teenager."

Jo Ann's mother offered another clue to the identity of at least one of the spirits who may be haunting the house from time to time. "My husband and I play cards quite a bit," she said, "and every once in a while, one of us will smell a strong odor of chewing tobacco just like the kind my father used to use. We always laugh and say, 'Hello, Pa!,' and the smell will last for five or ten minutes before drifting away. And since no one in our house smokes or uses tobacco, it's hard to say where else that smell could be coming from."

So the mystery remains, even though the number of peculiar incidents has lessened a great deal in recent years. The Heimers may never know who or what haunted their house, or why.

THE HAUNTING
OF
F.E. WARREN
AIR FORCE BASE

A fter Fort Laramie, the most haunted site in Wyoming is probably F.E. Warren Air Force Base on the outskirts of Cheyenne. Like Fort Laramie, Fort D.A. Russell, as it was originally called, was crucial to the state's and the nation's frontier history, and many of the thousands of men and women who have inhabited the site from then until now appear to be present even yet in one ghostly form or another.

Named after fallen Civil War hero David A. Russell, the fort was established in 1867. Its initial purpose was to protect the workers of the Union Pacific from Indian raids as they completed the United States' first transcontinental railroad. In later years, the fort aided migrants as they made their way west and served as a depot for the distribution of troops in the area.

In 1930 the name of the post was changed to Fort Francis E. Warren, in honor of the longtime senator and first governor of Wyoming. When the air force became a separate branch of the service in 1947, the army relinquished its jurisdiction of the fort, which was subsequently renamed the Francis E. Warren Air Force Base. In the 1980s, the base became best known for its deployment of Peacekeeper missiles.

132

With more than one hundred twenty years of such a varied history, it's no wonder that the base has been the site of many instances of psychic phenomena. But owing to the inherent secrecy of all military institutions, most of the stories at F.E. Warren are difficult to verify, and almost all are heard second- or thirdhand, at best.

The sheer number of tales is remarkable, however, especially since very few people have actually died at the base. Historic Preservation Officer Bill Metz has been collecting its spooky stories for quite some time, and one day he hopes to include all of them in an anthology.

"There have always been lots of sightings of ghosts in cavalry dress uniforms," Metz said, "and most of them occur in or near the earlier buildings. I'm sure you could get reports of hundreds of incidents if you talked to enough people.

"One of the best known happened a few years ago, when a family moved into a lovely old brick house on the base. On the very first night, their small daughter saw the silhouette of a cavalry officer standing in her playroom. From that time on, she refused to sleep in her bed unless the door to the adjoining playroom was closed."

Another ghost of a cavalry officer has been sighted by at least two men working in the Security Police Building. In the mid-1980s, Staff Sergeant with Law Enforcement Ed Davis had an encounter with this phantom at two or three o'clock one morning.

"People are always saying that your eyes play tricks on you, but I know what I saw," Davis insisted. "That officer was standing by one of the radiators, adjusting his trousers and boots. I said, 'Good evening,' and he said, 'Howdy.' Then it dawned on me that nobody else was supposed to be in that building, but by the time I turned around to get a better look, he had already vanished.

"He looked somewhat misty, but I'd say that he was middle-aged," Davis continued. "I don't know how to describe the shade of blue of his uniform, except to say that it was the color of the chalk on pool cues. That was a strange detail, because the actual uniforms weren't that color. But in every other way, the man was dressed like a cavalry officer of the 1800s, including the stripe down his pants. I didn't have a chance to observe his face very closely, but I did notice that he smiled when he spoke, and he seemed to be about five feet, seven inches tall."

A more recent sighting of the same ghost by a patrolman occurred in 1987. This man had photocopied some routine paperwork around six o'clock one morning, before anyone else had arrived. As he was walking down a dark hallway, he caught a glimpse of a man dressed in a cavalry uniform. The unexpected "visitor" apparently realized that he was being observed, for he bolted through an exit. The patrolman gave chase, but once outside the building, he found no one there.

Other phantoms from the days of Fort D.A. Russell include a captain who lived in what is now referred to as "The Ghost House" because of the frequency of sightings within it. One autumn day in the early years of this century, the captain was upstairs in the house entertaining his mistress. His family returned home unexpectedly; to avoid them, he climbed out of the second-story window, slipped on some ice, and fell to his death.

According to Bill Metz, within the last two years, residents of "The Ghost House" have reported seeing the captain in the area that used to be his office.

"One of them told me that he walked downstairs one night and found a light on; then he saw a man in early military dress seated at a desk. The resident of the house did a double take, but the captain vanished as quickly as he had appeared.

"Another ghost story has its origins in an indiscreet love affair that occurred a few years earlier, in the 1890s," Metz continued. "In this case, an officer had been seeing his mistress for quite some time when he suddenly transferred away from the base without telling her. She was so lovesick and despondent that she killed herself. Since then, people have seen her apparition wandering around the upstairs rooms of one of the houses."

Metz added that a wandering male ghost from approximately the same time period has been seen near the brick officers' quarters. "As the original wooden buildings burned to the ground, the enlisted men dashed in and out to salvage whatever they could," he explained. "One of them was trapped in the blaze and killed, and his phantom apparently still roams the area.

"Another story from the early days involves a woman who has been seen late at night visiting one of the graves in the old cemetery," Metz continued. "Three years ago, a security policeman told me that he had been making his rounds when he saw a veiled woman in black standing out in the graveyard. He parked his car to check on her, but when he walked to the spot where she had been, there was no one around, and no footprints were visible. He talked to some other security people, and several of them admitted having had the same experience.

"A lot of stories involve the security police," Metz explained, "because they're the only ones working in the early hours when many of the mysterious incidents take place. One of these fellows once walked around the corner of a building and was surprised to confront a soldier standing at attention on the edge of a field, just as if he were on guard. As the policeman approached the soldier, some clouds rolled in front of the moon. Seconds later, when the clouds had passed by and the moon was again shining brightly, the soldier had disappeared without a trace. But he had been standing in the location of the original Fort Russell guardhouse, the little shack near where the gate used to be.

"Probably the most dramatic apparition of all appeared to yet another security policeman who was driving out to check the missile sites," Metz added. "He looked up just in time to see an Indian in full Plains war regalia, charging across the prairie on a horse."

One of the more chilling stories from Fort Russell's past concerns an Indian woman who was raped and murdered by a small group of cavalry men at White Crow Creek, which is now the family camp area. Sergeant Ed Davis has heard the woman's terrified screams upon two occasions.

"Sometimes when I used to be on patrol in the morning," he said, "I would get calls from the guys in the barracks, saying that they could hear the screams of a woman out by the creek. I was never able to find anyone there, although I did hear her frantic cries. They were real enough to me that I think someone really did get raped and killed out there.

"In fact, several of us spent almost four hours one night, tearing that campground apart in order to find whoever was screaming," Davis admitted. "We could hear these terrible shrieks, but every time we ran toward them, the sound would shift so that they seemed to be coming from somewhere else. We finally had to give up, because we couldn't find anybody."

While such echoes from the fort's early days are responsible for a fair share of F.E. Warren's ghost stories, many of the eerie incidents reported today have origins which are unknown, or at best, uncertain.

"About ten years ago a family brought over a beautiful piano from Europe," Bill Metz remembered, "and late at night, they often heard an unseen someone playing it. In another story, a woman put a pot of soup on to simmer before she went shopping. When she got back, she found that all the knobs had been pulled off the stove and thrown into the kettle!"

One mischievous ghost used to roll a ball back and forth across an attic floor, and another especially nasty one cut up an artist's paintings and killed cats that lived on the premises. One can't help but wonder what would have happened if this ghost had met the feline phantom said to haunt a women's dorm.

"People have reported hearing this ghost for at least two decades, and the most recent experience was only a year or so ago," said Bill Metz. "The cat was supposed to have been smuggled in by one of the WACs shortly after World War II, and it became the dorm pet. One day it disappeared. Since then, the dorm residents have often heard a cat meowing in the hallway, but when they've opened their doors, there's nothing there. The entire dormitory has been searched from floor to ceiling, but no one has ever found any evidence of a cat in the building. Another version of the story is that the cat is from an even earlier time—that when the dorm was a cavalry barracks, the animal was the mascot."

Another ghostly cat, who resided in one of the brick houses, used to eat food set out for it, and it always left footprints across the family's piano. This animal was apparently attached to the people rather than to the location, though, since no one has reported any strange occurrences in the house since the family (and, presumably, their ghost cat) moved away.

The most famous animal ghost on the base, however, is the dog that served as an official mascot. "It lived in one of the men's dorms, and it was actually commissioned a sergeant," Bill Metz explained. "The dog was buried in the courtyard behind the dorm, and there are stories that on certain nights, it can still be heard barking to be let in. When the men in the dorm check around outside, however, there's never any animal in the vicinity."

Phantom pets don't usually cause anything worse than a temporary shiver down the spine, but if more serious psychic phenomena start causing problems, the detectives on the base conduct an investigation. Three or four years ago, they checked into some incidents that took place in one of the houses built in the 1960s. Kitchen drawers and cabinets were constantly flying open, and the front doorbell rang repeatedly even when no one was at the door. The father of the family soon began to keep the drawers and cabinets shut by jamming yardsticks and brooms under their handles, and he rationalized that the ringing doorbell was caused by the wind. No one was ever able to discover the cause of the disturbances, and after a while, they stopped by themselves.

Ghostly manifestations at F.E. Warren Air Force Base are certainly not restricted to people's homes, however. Many of the most commonly reported incidents today take place during working hours in institutional buildings. As Staff Sergeant John Spina admitted with a laugh, "All these weird things sort of make you not want to work in those places at night!"

The site of many hauntings, the Security Police Building was the base hospital until the 1960s, when it was converted to its present purpose. The building's former history clearly figures in at least a few of the psychic phenomena that have occurred there. Several people, including Sergeant Bert Johnson*, have witnessed an apparition who was most likely a family member visiting someone in the hospital.

"Back in 1980 or '81, another fellow and I climbed the stairs here in the police building, and we noticed something at the end of the hallway that at first looked hazy, like a cloud. Nothing registered with me at first, until my companion asked, 'Did you see that? It looked like a small girl!' I kept looking at the mist and decided that he was right. As we watched, the child appeared to be looking at us, and then she turned and walked toward a wall.

"She seemed to disappear into one of the offices at the end of the hallway, but when we checked, they were all locked up," Johnson said. "I didn't get a long enough look to be able to describe her, but I had seen enough to know that I didn't want to go back upstairs for quite a while!"

An enlisted man had the same response to a phantom he sighted near a soft drinks machine in the building. "I sent one of my men downstairs to get some colas, but he came running back in a few seconds without them," Sergeant Ed Davis explained. "I've never seen a person so pale in my entire life. When he could talk, he told us that he had been standing next to the soft drinks machine when he saw an old man sitting on one of those flip-topped metal garbage cans. When he said 'Hello' to the old man, he received no answer, and began walking toward him, wondering why he was so unfriendly. But before he got any closer, the old guy vanished in front of his eyes! The fellow who had this experience vowed never to go back down there again, and as far as I know, he never did."

Military working dogs, usually German shepherds, are trained to handle all kinds of dangerous situations, yet the ones at F.E. Warren have refused to go into the attic of the Security Police Building. One of them has also been reluctant to enter the third floor of the jail, the building once used for medical emergencies.

"Nobody knew why it acted that way," said Davis, "but that dog literally had to be carried onto the third floor! And it wasn't the only one to be bothered by something up there. An officer who is no longer here once ordered an elevator in the building to be locked and never used again. Apparently he had entered it on the third floor, and as he pushed the button to take him down, the doors opened and he felt someone get in, push him aside, and ride with him to the lowest level of the building."

Could this ghost also be responsible for opening and closing the door of the jail?

"Another fellow and I were studying in an office one morning around two or three o'clock," Davis explained, "and we distinctly heard the door of the jail open and close. There was no mistaking what we had heard, because the jail door makes a very distinctive sound. The next thing we knew, footsteps started down the hallway toward us. I couldn't see anything, but I'll never forget the casual pace and the clicking of those invisible heels. They didn't stop until they were right in front of me, and the guy with me said, 'You've got to wish him a good evening.' I looked at my companion as if he were crazy, but he said, 'You've got to say something!' Finally, just to humor my friend, I said, 'Good evening,' and I heard the sound of someone in cowboy boots walking away from me. Next, I heard that same distinctive sound of the jail door opening up, but I saw that the door itself never opened. I looked over at my friend in disbelief, and he told me that we had just been paid a visit by the ghost of a doctor who used to be on base!

"I'm a firm believer that we *do* have the spirit of a doctor here in the jail," Davis explained. "He's never shown himself, but he certainly makes his presence known!

"For one thing, he rearranges the furniture in the rec room so that one chair is always right in front of the television. I used to think that my guards were playing tricks on me, because every time I set that chair to the side, the next day it would be right back where it had been, smack dab in front of the TV set.

"The ghost has made it clear that that is his place, so we humor him by not sitting in his chair. Several times I've been sitting on the couch watching TV when I've felt a cold draft enter the room. Then it's as if someone walks over and sits on that chair—you can even see the cushion go down! Right about then the TV channel changes, and that's when I get out of there as fast as I can!

"At first we thought that some kind of outside interference was making the channel change, but you can actually see the button on the remote control unit go down, just as if an invisible finger were pushing it. And no matter what program anyone is watching, the ghost always changes over to the Lifetime channel, the one with all the medical news. That's why we think he must have been a doctor.

"Just the other night, a bodybuilder who stands about six-four came running out of that room and said, 'I'm not going back in there unless somebody goes with me!' You could tell that something had really scared him.

"We think that the channel-changing doctor is also the one who plays games with the prisoners in the jail," Davis continued. "The men are locked in rooms with heavy doors, and the only way to get in or out is with the keys that the guards have. But many times, the prisoners have been unable to find their shoes in the morning, even though they had placed them in their own cells the night before.

The guards swear that they have not been playing tricks on us, and that after the prisoners are asleep, the keys usually go into a box which is locked inside another of the offices. Time and again, however, all the missing shoes have shown up in another prisoner's cell, and they're neatly lined up, not just thrown in carelessly.

"We've got another prankster on the law enforcement desk who loves to get fresh with women," Davis added. "One night a female sergeant was working there by herself, and something kept knocking and tapping on the walls around her. She felt a sensation as if someone were coming up behind her and blowing on her ear and neck, but she tried not to let it bother her, because she couldn't see anything. One night, however, whatever it was kissed her on the nape of the neck, and she put out a call for help on the radio.

"She sounded frightened, so we came in, guns loaded and ready for action; and there she stood in a corner, shivering like crazy. Something had obviously scared the living daylights out of her, and she refused to work that desk by herself after that. Another woman later said that the same thing had happened to her, but she had just put it down to bugs crawling on her!

"Nobody has had any experiences with our kissing ghost for quite some time now," Davis concluded, "maybe because we remodeled the law enforcement desk, or maybe because we don't have women working there by themselves anymore."

Much more frightening than the attacks of the phantom kisser, however, was the ordeal undergone by a young woman who lived with her toddler in a house on the base. In 1986, Sheila Monroe* woke up in the middle of the night to see a man standing in the doorway of her bedroom. He stared at her, said nothing, and vanished after a few seconds. The young woman told herself that she had been dreaming, until the same thing happened the next night. This time, however, a woman had joined the man in Sheila's bedroom doorway, and both of them stood and stared speechlessly at her.

Sheila became frightened and threw a pillow at the apparitions, who immediately disappeared. Afraid to spend another night alone, she asked a neighbor over to sleep on the couch in the living room. Nothing happened the first night, but on the second, the man on the couch heard footsteps coming from the bedroom toward the living room, and assumed that they were Sheila's until someone or something grabbed his ankles and jerked him off the couch. Scrambling to his feet again, he turned on the lights to find himself alone in the room.

On the next night, Sheila woke up to find not only the man and the woman, but a child as well, standing in her bedroom doorway as before. She screamed and threw the pillow, once again causing the ghosts to disappear.

The nightmare had only started, however, for as Sheila began sobbing from nervous exhaustion, she heard her baby screaming in terror down the hall. She ran toward the child's bedroom and twisted the knob, but some incredibly strong force kept her from opening the door.

Panic-stricken, Sheila heard her baby's frantic wailing and the sounds of pictures being ripped from the walls and falling onto the desk and floor. Only when the child stopped crying could the distraught mother get the door open.

Her heart jumped in relief when she saw that her baby was safe in its crib, but the room was a shambles, as if a whirlwind had passed through and blown everything from its place. Oddest of all was a poster that had been removed carefully from the wall, the tacks lying beside it on the floor. This episode convinced Sheila that she needed outside help to stop the terrifying phenomena occurring in her home.

She contacted investigators at the base, who came the next evening. Sergeant Larry Mitchell was one of them, and his initial reaction was disbelief, although he, too, was completely mystified by what happened next.

"My partner got a couple guys together, and they were all going to spend the night there to see what was going on," Sergeant Mitchell recalled. "Around one or two o'clock in the morning, they fell asleep—two guys on couches and another one on the floor of the living room. After half an hour or so, the guy on the floor started writhing around and couldn't breathe. My partner jumped up from the couch and calmed him down, and when he did, the fellow on the floor explained that he had been awake the whole time, but he had felt someone shutting off his breath by stepping on his chest.

"By this time, my partner was convinced that something was definitely going on, but I still had my doubts. After all, the woman might have been making all this up because she wanted to be transferred to a better house, and the investigators could have been unduly influenced by her hysteria. But my partner went to interview the previous tenant, and he reported having had some of the same things happen to him. He had seen no apparitions, but he did have a terrible feeling in bed one night that someone was trying to squeeze into his body with him. And he had food disappear from his refrigerator—he'd take a steak out to thaw, but when he came back to cook it, it would be gone!

"Sheila also began missing food occasionally, some pork chops once, and milk another time. And sometimes she would leave the windows shut and locked, and when she got home, they would be halfway up.

"After I saw more of her, I became convinced that she was telling the truth," Mitchell said. "She even went to a psychiatrist, who confirmed that whatever she was relating, she believed to be true; and when she talked to a chaplain on the base, he told her that her story was a classic case of haunting.

"But the most amazing part of the story is yet to come," Mitchell promised. "We took a detailed description of the three apparitions that Sheila had seen, and talked to the man who used to own the house, as well as neighbors. We found out that the descriptions of the ghosts are exactly those of a family that lived in the house a few years ago! When they left here, they moved to Alaska, where all three of them were killed in a car accident.

"Once we found this out, the disturbances quit immediately, and they've never returned. I still don't believe too much in ghosts, but I don't have any other explanation for what happened, either. And why the manifestations seemed malicious is also unclear, since it seems that all the family really wanted was for us to know what had happened to them."

Could this simple need to be acknowledged be behind the majority of hauntings that seem pointless otherwise? Certainly, a great deal of the psychic phenomena occurring at F.E. Warren Air Force Base (and elsewhere) would seem to have no other purpose but to link the spirits of the dead with the living, in case we forget those who have gone before.

THE APPARITION
OF
JOHN D. MARTIN

A chilling tale set in a coal mining camp at the turn of the century comes from the files of the Wyoming State Historical Association. Titled simply "A Ghost Story," the account by Breta B. Morrow was written on October 25, 1938, about forty years after the strange event it describes.

When Breta was approximately ten years old, her father, Joseph Bird, Sr., was the state coal mine inspector, and the family lived a mile from Oakley in the southwest corner of Wyoming. Each day, Breta's twenty-year-old sister Beatrice walked the three miles into Kemmerer for sewing and millinery lessons, often accompanied by her friend Martha Purdy.

One night, Bea stopped to have supper at Martha's house before returning home. After washing the dishes, the two young women visited and played the piano until around nine-thirty, when Martha began walking Bea to her residence outside of town.

John D. Martin, a pathetic soul who for some reason was always referred to by his full name, was at that time one of the workers at the mine in Oakley. Because of his eccentric manner and his recent release from the Evanston hospital for the mentally ill, many townsfolk feared the misfit while others ridiculed him. He was best known for his "goofy" grin and his disconcerting habit of gawking at everyone he met.

On the night in question, Bea and Martha had approached the bridge that spanned the Hams Fork River in Oakley. Someone appeared to be standing on the structure, but as the two women drew nearer, whoever it was suddenly evaporated before their eyes.

"Did you see that?" one of them asked as soon as she could catch her breath.

The other replied that it was certainly a ghost, and the last thing either wanted to do was to walk across the bridge. Wasting no time, they retraced their steps to Martha's house.

As they had expected, Martha's brothers laughed when they heard the story, but they did consent to accompany them to Bea's residence. This time, as the group of young people crossed the bridge, there was no one else even near it.

Upon reaching the Bird home about ten-thirty, Bea and Martha repeated their story that they had seen someone on the bridge. Mrs. Bird laughed along with Martha's brothers and said, "Oh, it was just old John D. Martin again, following you."

A little later that same evening, Mr. Bird received a telephone call. There had been an accident at the mine and John D. Martin had been killed.

"See, I told you," Mrs. Bird persisted jokingly when she heard the news. "It was John D. Martin that you saw tonight—that must have been his ghost!"

The family all looked at each other, and Bea's eyes opened wide. From that moment, she was certain that what she had seen was the unfortunate man's apparition.

Morrow concludes the anecdote with a statement made by her sister many years after the incident took place. Bea's ambivalent assessment of what she saw is typical of all sensible, rational people who don't believe in the supernatural but are hard pressed for any other explanation as to what they have encountered.

"I don't believe in ghosts," she maintained. "I know there are no such things, but I know I saw a ghost that night, and I will never be able to think it was anything else."

"THEY WANT US
TO KNOW
THEY'RE STILL HERE!"

E ncountering a ghost in broad daylight is disconcerting enough, and most of us would quake in our shoes at the approach of even a friendly phantom. Imagine, then, how you would feel about a dark-eyed specter who paid nocturnal visits to your bed with the express purpose of wrapping its hands about your throat and choking the breath from you as you slept!

This isn't the theme of an old Vincent Price movie, or a new plot twist in the *Nightmare on Elm Street* sequence—it's what really happened to the Lyle family of Rawlins, Wyoming.

Nancy Lyle awoke one night in 1982 with a terrible pressure on her neck. "I couldn't get any air," she recalled with a shudder, "and I couldn't even call out for help to my husband who was lying beside me. All I could do was to thrash my arms around until he awoke. Finally, he stirred a little and sat up, and as he did so, a small wisp of something like smoke moved from the bed and out into another room."

For a long time, Nancy didn't mention her nighttime ordeal to anyone. Then, on a trip to visit her sister in Illinois, she finally shared her experience with the family. "My sister almost fainted," Nancy said, "because the same thing had happened to her when she visited our house the year before. She and her husband had been sleeping in that same bed, and she also felt the pressure around her throat. She had never dared tell anybody, because she thought no one would believe her!"

Nancy's daughters both had similarly nightmarish episodes. The older one had returned from college and was sleeping in a room directly across from the one where her mother and aunt had been choked. Waking up to find herself surrounded by small white spinning whirlwinds, she fled in terror and refused to stay in the room again. Younger daughter Becky's incident more closely paralleled her mother's, as she felt something holding her shoulders down in bed one morning.

"I remember hearing stories to the effect that if you tell the devil you're not afraid, he will go away," Becky explained. "But my voice just wouldn't come out, so I kept thinking, 'I'm not afraid of you. Get out of here!' And the pressure stopped. Just when I decided I had been dreaming, however, it started all over again. Some people have told us that we must have been imagining the whole thing, but I don't believe that. When you're being choked or forcibly held down, you're not imagining it. If you can't breathe, you can't breathe. It's as simple as that."

"Several other unnerving things also happened," Nancy interjected. "My husband sometimes works nights, so I'm often asleep when he gets home. One night I felt him getting into bed, so I reached my leg over to touch his. His skin was very cold, and I remember thinking that he must have had to work outside. Content that he was home safely, I rolled over to go back to sleep. Then, just a few minutes later, I heard him coming through the front door!

"Another time when he worked late," Nancy continued, "I rolled over and saw something so vivid that I can still see it in my mind to this day. Staring at me from the other pillow was a face that looked like that of an American Indian. It had long, dark hair skinned back, with black warpaint smudged around the eyes.

"You can see why I used to dread going to bed," Nancy explained. "Each night, I'd make the sign of the cross with my hands and say every prayer I could think of. We also heard that you could write to spirits, so we used to drop notes saying 'Please go away and leave us alone!' down the stairway. Many times I've slept with the light on. I was grateful just to be able to get through the night without something happening."

Nancy's teenaged son Brian was also the target for the hostile advances of the mysterious fiend. "One night I was sleeping with my hand up by my head, when something grabbed my wrist and jerked me into a sitting position," he remembered. "That was the most petrified I've ever been in my life. I had no idea what was going on—I felt completely powerless. I tried to scream, but nothing would come out. I tried to free myself, but I was paralyzed; and whatever had ahold of me was the strongest physical force I've ever felt. I saw a big, white, shapeless blob that eventually let go of me and floated quickly out of the room. It was like a very bright light, but it didn't hurt my eyes, even though I looked right at it. I couldn't sleep the rest of the night after that happened!"

Brian's sleep was to be disturbed by other, equally terrifying manifestations. "I was an artist in high school," he continued, "and one night when I was getting ready for bed, it looked as though someone picked up one of my sculptures and bounced it about two feet off of my desk. And then some drawings that were propped against the wall began to move, and to slide back and forth across the floor. I took off running and didn't go back for the rest of the night!

"That reminds me of something else that happened every day for about a month or so," he said. "I found that I didn't have to set my alarm, because every morning, something would come right up and punch me in the back of the head so that my head would actually move across the pillow. It was painful, and it scared me until I got used to it. And every time I turned around to look, I caught a glimpse of something or someone sitting on a little TV in my room, looking out the window. I don't know what the heck it was!

"Another time, I was downstairs lifting weights. I was lying down on the bench with the bar in position to lift my legs and thighs. When I finished with it, the bar wouldn't go back down; and as I sat up, a suitcase sitting four or five feet from the bench suddenly slid across the floor, moving right under my feet and the bench, too.

"Something just as weird happened while I was eating breakfast one morning," Brian added. "I was the only one in the house, and I had finished my cereal, so I was spinning a quarter and trying to shoot it into a cup. The quarter fell off the table, so I left it there when I went to put my bowl in the sink. When I came back, the coin was on the table again!

"Sometimes we see a chair rocking with no one in it," he said, "and lots of times, things disappear from where we've put them. On several occasions, I've had the channels change on me while I'm watching TV, and many times we've all felt an invisible someone sitting down on our beds or walking across them."

—

More than once, in fact, Brian's formerly skeptical father has felt someone sit on his bed, and when he reached for his wife, he was surprised to find no one there.

The Lyles believe that the strange things occurring in their home may have much in common with the poltergeist phenomenon. Certainly some of the occurrences seem to point to psychokinetic energy as a possible solution. Consider the glass of Kool-aid that overturned when Nancy looked at it from across the room, or the time she was listening to a tape of Dolly Parton and heard a deep male voice come on at the end to ask "What's next?" She was certain she had never heard it before, and when she immediately played back the tape for her children, there was no trace of any voice but the singer's.

An even more bizarre incident happened to Becky. "Mine is a corner bedroom with doors on two sides," she said. "One day, I saw my sister come in one door and say something to me; then she went out that same door. To go out, then to come back in through the other door requires going clear around the house. And yet, about two seconds after I saw her come in the first door, she knocked on the second and came in through that. I've never been able to figure out what happened. The first time, she couldn't have really been there, so what did I see? Her ghost?"

It's possible, of course, that Becky is mistaken, and that her sister could have come in one door and out the other before popping back in through the same one she had exited. If Becky hadn't been paying particularly close attention to her sister's coming and going, she might not have realized which doors her sister used in the sequence.

Oddly enough, people can frequently be fooled by appearances in this way, but animals rarely can. That something peculiar was going on in the Lyle house was borne out by the behavior of a cat, now deceased, that would anxiously run and claw at Nancy's feet, as if to prevent her going downstairs. At other times, the cat sat at the top of the steps and hissed in fear at the unseen evils below him.

"For years we didn't talk about what was going on to anyone outside of our family or close friends," Nancy said. "But then Becky had a class with one of our neighbor's daughters and found out that they had had similar activity in their house.

"Sue, the mother, had a sewing room upstairs, and her husband had built a pegboard to hold her spools of thread. One day when she was in there sewing, she had a strange feeling, so she turned around to see the spools coming off the pegs and floating across the room!

"And their animals acted just like our cat did—every time Sue tried to go downstairs, they would throw themselves in front of her, grab her and pull at her to keep her from leaving the room.

"The spookiest thing that ever happened took place during Christmastime," Nancy continued. "They had a stereo and a pair of large speakers on the wall, and as Sue was sitting in the room, the speakers suddenly moved away from the wall and stood straight out with their electrical cords as taut as wire. They remained that way for a second before crashing to the floor.

"Another night, Sue and one of her daughters were standing at the sink doing dishes, when all the crockery in the cupboard started shaking and rattling for no reason."

Is the fact that two adjacent households have experienced paranormal phenomena merely a coincidence, or is there a connection between them? The Lyles believe that there is, and that the connection extends also to the Rawlins Middle School close by.

"We're only one block and a field from the school," Nancy explained, "and one of the janitors told me that he had talked to some very elderly people who were born and raised here, and who believed that this entire area was once a burial ground. Since all these things have happened to us, we've tried to come up with theories, and nothing made sense until we realized that the building of the school might have stirred things up. The house was only about a year old when we moved there in the mid-1970s, and nothing unusual occurred until 1980, by which time the school had been constructed and was already in use."

Rumors are rife but conflicting about the supposed burial ground that was disturbed, and my repeated attempts to contact the construction company failed. Former middle school principals Don Blakeslee and Don Woodley were aware of the rumor, as practically everyone in town seemed to be, but they both claimed that nothing in the records indicated that there had ever been a burial ground at the site, and that as far as they knew, no grave sites were ever discovered during the excavation.

More confusion exists concerning the type of graveyard it was supposed to be. The prevailing gossip is that it was an Indian burial ground, perhaps even an ancient one, but a janitor at the school claims to know that it was a white cemetery. "I know the guy who took the caskets out," he said. "He told me he took out three, but the rest were all mangled, so he just left them. Nobody will believe him now, though, since he went to prison for drugs."

A theory held by fellow janitor Agneda Esquibel is that the graveyard may be the resting place of pioneers who died on a wagon train headed for Casper. It's true that the anonymous graves of would-be settlers dot the plains and prairies throughout the West, and this fact may explain why no records exist pertaining to the site.

Whether the school and the houses were built on a burial ground or not, quite a few of the custodians of Rawlins Middle School are convinced that the place is haunted—one so much so that he quit his job rather than work nights! Another janitor, who had the greatest number of eerie experiences, was so frightened by what he had seen and heard that he refused to be interviewed. Becky Lyle, however, had heard one of his stories and repeated it to me.

"Because of all the scary things going on in the school, this particular janitor decided to bring his dogs to work," she said. "He saw a light coming from a room that should have been dark, so he went to investigate and found a woman standing there. She turned and began walking away before she finally faded completely. The janitor went back to get his dogs, who refused to go inside the room where the apparition had been. Instead, they barked furiously as though something were still there."

Most of the stories concern this lady, always dressed in white, who has been seen in various parts of the building. One janitor relayed the secondhand report that a patrolman who was checking the rooms once beamed his flashlight on the ghostly woman, who immediately disappeared. Another story is that a custodian was walking by the science room when he looked inside to see the lady floating up against the window. Upon another occasion, the same man observed her walking into the gym and turning into the boys' locker room. When he followed her, he found the room empty.

Agneda Esquibel saw another phantom on one of her nightly rounds. "At about eight-thirty one night, I came out of the bathrooms and saw a man standing in the hallway," she said. "I didn't see his face, but he was wearing a nice-looking black suit with a white shirt. He was quite short, about five feet tall, and neither skinny nor fat. From what I saw of him, he appeared to be young, and his clothing looked modern. I assumed he was looking for somebody in the school, although it did seem odd for him to be there so late in the evening. I asked him, 'Can I help you?' in both Spanish and English, but I got no response. Then he began running away from me and I followed, wondering what in the world he was doing. As he got to the music room, he turned slightly and then I noticed—he didn't have a head! When I had first seen him, even though I couldn't see his face, he at least had had a head; but when I saw him again, he was without it. He kept running and then just disappeared.

"You should have seen me bolt out of there! I headed over to the gym, where I told the other custodians what I had seen. I insisted that they call the police, because I thought the man might still be hiding in the area. The cops came and we all went looking, but found no trace of him. I'm usually not scared of things like that, but this man was like the devil!

"That was the only time I've seen a ghost at the school," Agneda confessed, "although sometimes I've caught glimpses of something shadowy out of the corners of my eyes. Other strange things have happened, too. One night I was vacuuming the music room, and I heard somebody knocking on the door. I turned to look but didn't see anyone, so I started vacuuming again—when suddenly, someone pulled the plug right out of the socket! I called out, 'Who's playing around with me?' and went to check both the hall and the band room, but nobody was there."

As recently as 1988, Agneda became the victim of another ghostly prank involving her vacuum cleaner. "I had straightened out the big and small cords to wash them," she explained. "As I was washing the big one, however, I saw the little one creeping up by itself toward the vacuum, just as if someone were pulling it!"

Agneda has also heard doors open and close when no one is there, as well as the sounds of an invisible someone walking back and forth on the three stair steps leading from the music room to the band room. Eddie Vialpndo, another custodian, has witnessed a shadowy figure darting around a corner of a long hallway, and another time he heard loud, unexplained pounding on a wall in the gym area.

Although these kinds of things still happen occasionally, most of the disturbances have died down now, both in the Rawlins Middle School and in the homes of the Lyles and their neighbors. According to Nancy Lyle, in fact, the neighbors who experienced the psychic phenomena have moved away, and the new owners of the property have reported nothing out of the ordinary.

The Lyles, too, are a lot less jumpy these days. "Since the last year and a half, I haven't felt uneasy in the house," Nancy said. "I no longer feel afraid when I go downstairs, and although we still feel someone sitting on the bed now and then, it doesn't bother me anymore. Of course, my husband works days mostly now, too, and I feel better knowing he's there, so I can ask him 'Did you feel that?' when we have our bedroom visitor."

If the Lyles and the custodians at the Rawlins Middle School have finally begun to accept the weird phenomena that once terrorized them, they have come but little closer to understanding them. But perhaps the explanation is as straightforward as Becky Lyle suggested it might be.

"Maybe the haunting *is* caused by the spirits of people who are buried close by," she said, "but I don't think they've ever meant to do real harm—if they had wanted to, they could have choked us all to death! But I think that the spirits themselves are just trying to get attention. They're just reminding us that they're still here!"

THE PIONEER WOMAN'S STORY

S adie Evalena Hale and her husband Dudley were late-nineteenth-century settlers on Luman Creek, at the very foot of the Bighorn Mountains of north central Wyoming. After living for short periods of time in Terry, Montana, and Sheridan, Wyoming, the couple and their two daughters set out for the Bighorns, and eventually built their dream mountain home after filing on what had been a very badly cut up parcel of approximately ten acres. At the back of their property was an abrupt high rocky ledge, and lying in front was a lesser one, so in between the two the Hales built the three-room rough log cabin that must have seemed palatial at the time, in spite of the dirt floors and the flour sacks that covered the windows until glass could replace them.

The Hales were the first settlers to build on the stream, and it wasn't long before their home became a pleasant oasis. Fed entirely by springs, Luman Creek furnished a ready water supply that the Hales used to grow alfalfa, corn, small grains, strawberries, and plenty of garden vegetables. So rich were their harvests that in the fall when the Hales went into nearby Hyattville, they often loaded up their wagon with watermelons to give to the citizens of the town. And to add a touch of beauty to her garden, Mrs. Hale tended the cheerfully towering hollyhocks, grown from seeds she had brought from Montana.

Natural food supplies were also plentiful near the Hales' new home. Currants, wild cherries, giant gooseberries, raspberries, and buffalo berries grew wild in the bushes along Luman Creek, and trout were so lazy that the two little girls, Rosa and Jeanette Mary, often captured them by hand and then surprised their parents by bringing them home for supper. In addition, a few cows and hogs and a flock of chickens provided the family with all they needed to create an Eden out of the wilderness.

But trouble arises even in the most pleasant of places. One night while she was preparing supper, Mrs. Hale became seriously ill, and she sent her uncle to bring home her husband, who was doing carpenter work six miles away for J.J. Smith. Mrs. Hale's condition worsened, and her suffering became even harder to bear.

Mr. Hale's chief employment had been as irrigator for John Luman, and later he had charge of Luman's herd of cattle. When Mrs. Hale became critically ill, Curt Simmons, Luman's bookkeeper, informed the couple of a lady visiting the area who was reputed to have great powers of healing. Because she was so close and the nearest medical doctor was as far away as Basin, the Hales gave their permission for Simmons to go and get her.

When he returned, he brought with him a woman dressed entirely in black, who took Mrs. Hale's hand in her own as soon as she entered the room. At that very instant, Sadie Hale felt a mysterious power surge throughout her body. Then, as she was temporarily strengthened, she told the lady in black to go have her supper, as Mr. Hale would stay with her.

"Do you remember, Dud, the strange dream I told you of, a year ago?" Mrs. Hale asked him. "Of the woman totally in black standing beside my bed, holding my hand?"

"I sure do," answered Mr. Hale. "It was a dream you thought a great deal about, but couldn't connect with any previous thought."

"Dud," Mrs. Hale continued, "this is that woman! I remember that face, the all black outfit, and she took my hand. Only one thing isn't right. In my dream she came into the yard in a shiny black-topped buggy, but Mr. Simmons went after her in a lumber wagon."

"No," Dud corrected her. "It fits in that detail, too. He went down to Luman and got John's new buggy. He thought it would be so much faster in making the trip."

"I do declare!" was all Mrs. Hale could say.

The family continued to watch over her anxiously for several more days, because she remained critically ill. But the lady in black never wavered in her efforts to bring Mrs. Hale back to good health. She cast herself in a trance and massaged the invalid from head to toe, slapping her body smartly until she glowed. Mrs. Hale had never seen anything like it, and came to believe that her mysterious friend was not a nurse, but a spiritualist. Thinking about the strange practices of the lady in black, Mrs. Hale at one point laughed out loud.

"You laugh, go right ahead! It's good for you!" the lady said, encouraged by Mrs. Hale's good humor. She continued her strange healing rituals, muttering to herself at times and remaining in perfect quiet trances at others, never giving up on her patient.

But Mrs. Hale's suffering continued, until she was finally comforted by her belief that the ease of death was not far away. No longer could she continue to struggle for life, even though her two little girls and her husband loved and needed her desperately. But just at the time she felt closest to death, she heard an insistent voice nearby, saying "You are not going to die. We are not going to let you die."

Mrs. Hale was never able to tell later just how much time passed between hearing the voice and hearing a great "Whew-w-w-w" sound that signalled the end of her illness. Tumbling one over another were great white clouds that rolled from her head down the length of her body and off the foot of the bed. She looked up to see her husband, leaning on the mantle with his head down and his face pale as a ghost.

"Dud, what's the matter?" she asked.

"Thank God, she'll live!" He spoke as if in answer to prayer.

The lady in black stayed for three more weeks while Mrs. Hale continued her recovery. One day the two women were looking through Mrs. Hale's family photograph album. The lady in black pointed to one of the pictures.

"I know this lady," she said.

"Oh, but you don't," Mrs. Hale explained. "She's been dead a great many years. That's my mother, who died when I was two."

"But I do know her," the lady insisted. "She has been right here beside you and me during all your sickness. She spoke to you. She said, 'You're not going to die. We won't let you die.' "

"I thought you said that!" Mrs. Hale replied in astonishment.

"No, that was your mother," maintained the lady in black.

Years later, Sadie Evalena Hale Blake still marveled at the strangeness of the events leading to her recovery. On June 25, 1941, she granted a lengthy interview (from a part of which this chapter is closely drawn) to Basin schoolteacher Verda Burnham as part of a W.P.A. project on early settlers. "I never had any faith in such things," she said, "and yet this was an experience, true, exactly as I've related it here."

What are we to make of Mrs. Hale's story? May we assume from it that the spirits of the dead are able to return to help their loved ones still on earth?

THE EXTRAORDINARY
TALE OF
CHIEF BLACK FOOT

P robably the best-publicized and most incredible of all Wyoming ghost stories, the tale of Chief Black Foot had its beginning in September 1975 in the bedroom of the Reverend Victoria Mauricio, a Virginia Beach, Virginia, psychic.

"One night I awoke suddenly to the sound of loud drumming," the Reverend Mauricio recalled. "But instead of finding myself in the familiar surroundings of my room, I discovered to my confusion and horror that I had been buried up to my neck in dirt on a prairie. Grass was tickling my neck, and I couldn't find my husband, who had been sleeping peacefuliy next to me only moments before. I was utterly terrified that he had been buried alive and that a similar fate awaited me. I looked up to see the night sky, but oddly enough, I could still feel my French provincial bed behind my head.

"The drums became louder as I watched a group of Indians smearing warpaint on their faces and sharpening knives, getting ready to scalp me, no doubt. I tried to scream, but not a sound would come from my constricted throat. The angry Indians began to dance around a fire, moving closer and closer to me all the time.

"Suddenly, from out of nowhere, a huge Indian in buckskin pants and a breech cloth jumped into the dancers' midst with a large tomahawk in his hand. He yelled, 'Peace, brothers, not war!' and the others picked up their paint pots and knives and fled.

"Then this enormous man approached me, still holding the tomahawk. His black braids hung nearly to his waist, and his upper body was naked except for a string of beads around his neck. As he stood over me, I remember thinking that any second I would feel the sting of his tomahawk slicing right through my skull!

"Instead, he put one gigantic foot on either side of me, looked into my eyes, and said, 'I am Black Foot, I am a Crow Indian, I am your guardian angel. Do not be afraid; I'm here to protect you. This tomahawk will be a sign between you and me. I shall be back to talk to you. Do not be afraid.'

"At the end of his brief speech, the room spun around, Black Foot was gone, and I found myself back in my bed as if nothing had happened. My husband was still next to me, snoring gently, and instead of being afraid, I felt protected by the Chief."

The Reverend Mauricio is certain that her experience was neither a dream nor a vision, but an actual event. Born in South Wales into a psychic family, she has often experienced similar changes of scene. "Spirits are very creative, and I'm very creative, too," she explained, "and I'm sure that in my subconscious state of mind, Chief Black Foot placed me into the earth before waking me up. Over the years, I've had many things change completely before my eyes.

"As he had promised, the Chief kept coming back to me, and in the spring of 1976, he sent me to 'the room of books,' which was, of course, the local library. I gathered together all the volumes on Plains Indians, and after several hours, I found what I was looking for. There, in a picture of five Crow Indians, the man seated second from the left was identified as Chief Black Foot. In his hands he held the tomahawk which was our special sign!

"One day he came to me and said that it was time for me to get in touch with his people, and with that, he vanished. As he was leaving, I cried out, 'But where are they?' and I heard him answer, 'You find out.'

"At first, I had no idea where to begin," the Reverend Mauricio confessed. "I was unsuccessful in finding much information about the Crows at the local library, so I visited a psychic center there at Virginia Beach. The librarian at this institution gave me a newspaper called *Akwasasne Notes*, published by the Mohawk Nation, so I called their telephone number and discovered that the Crow Indians lived near Billings, Montana."

Victoria Mauricio's next step was to try to convince Clara White Hip, the woman answering the phone at the Crow Agency of the Bureau of Indian Affairs, that she was not just another prankster. "Apparently the reservation gets wacky phone calls all the time," she explained, "so you can imagine what she thought when I told her, 'Hey, listen, I'm a psychic who has been talking with a Crow Indian who appears to me regularly.' "

It took almost six months of calling before the Reverend Mauricio could get anyone to take her seriously. No one at the reservation seemed even to have heard of Chief Black Foot. One day, however, the Chief gave the psychic a message for the Crow Agency, that he was concerned with the desecration of graves of Indians. Upon hearing this, Clara White Hip spoke to the Crow historian, who informed her that Black Foot was indeed a very important chief, the Mountain Crow leader who had headed the Indian representatives at the signing of the Treaty of Fort Laramie. Among other things, this treaty established the Crow reservation boundary and provided for laws to be made by the majority of the tribe and not just by the chiefs.

The historian also explained that the Chief was better known to his own people as Sits-In-The-Middle-Of-The-Land, that Black Foot was the name given him by white soldiers in honor of his killing so many of the Blackfoot Indians, the great enemy of the Crows. He was presumed to have been born in the Absaroka range around 1795, and he died in his early eighties, when he and his wife went on a hunting expedition in the autumn of 1877. Both of them developed pneumonia, died within a day of each other, and were supposedly buried together in a cave somewhere near Cody, Wyoming.

Victoria Mauricio's contact with the Chief continued. One day not long after receiving the historical information about him, she was standing outside a department store when his voice commanded her to do an odd thing. He wanted her to buy an entire basket full of small packages in the women's clothing section of a nearby shop. A sign on the counter proclaimed that the little bundles contained silver charms, reduced from five dollars to ten cents apiece. Hastening to obey the Chief, the psychic bought them and hurried home.

In her book, *The Return of Chief Black Foot* (Virginia Beach, Virginia: The Donning Company, 1981, 7), the Reverend Mauricio described her amazement when she saw what she had purchased. "The first packet I opened held a miniature tomahawk, the second charm was a miniature peace pipe, then the shaman stick, a Plains tree, and a miniature music box (Black Foot said he liked the white man's music) which represented to him the music he heard on the

Plains those many years ago. I was dumbfounded to get all Indian charms."

She was even more dumbfounded when she returned to the store to try to get duplicates for her stepmother in England. She was told quite firmly that the store did not have Indian charms, but that if it did, they would certainly be in the jewelry section rather than in women's wear. Victoria Mauricio believes that the charms were a gift from the Chief, who wanted to prove that he was still with her.

He proved himself to the former skeptics at the Crow Agency, too, when he helped them locate two missing persons. "One day Clara called to tell me about a woman whose grown son had disappeared. She asked whether Black Foot would help to find him, and as soon as I hung up the phone, he told me that the man was not dead, that he was forty miles from his home, and that he was an epileptic. Apparently there had been a family dispute just before he ran away. The part that amazed the young man's mother the most was that I knew he was an epileptic, since that had always been a well-guarded family secret."

Another time, the Chief was called upon to find a two-year-old girl who was missing. "The reservation psychic said she was wandering in the woods, but a sorrowful Chief Black Foot said no, she had drowned," Victoria Mauricio said. "Searchers were looking up and down a stretch of the river, but the Chief said that she would be found a mile in the other direction, near three tall trees floating in the water, and her mouth would be full of mud. And that's exactly how they found her.

"When the searchers called me back, they asked, 'Can you really prove to us that Chief Black Foot was here? Can he tell us how she was dressed?' And he said, 'Yes, in red and white,' and then they were satisfied that he really *had* been with them.

"The Chief soon let me know that he wanted me to visit his people on the reservation," the Reverend Mauricio continued. "I didn't know why, but he kept repeating something that sounded like 'Tse-Tse,' and I wondered if there were cases of sleeping sickness in Africa that he wanted me to know about, so that I could notify the authorities. I couldn't see any connection to the reservation, but in seances he was most insistent upon my going. My husband of thirty years had recently died of a stroke, and as soon as the estate was settled and I could get away, I made the trip, on July 11, 1978."

Victoria Mauricio had been on the reservation for four days when the Chief suddenly appeared at her bedside. "He said to me, 'Do you know why I brought you out here?' and I said that I didn't. Then he told me that his bones had been buried on white man's land,

and that he wanted them brought back to be with his own people. He told me to find a shaman, or medicine man; so that's when I contacted Francis Stewart, a Crow Indian who had had a Scottish great grandfather, to lead the search for the remains."

The mystery of why the Chief had singled out a Welsh-born woman from Virginia to relay his messages was also explained during the Reverend Mauricio's first trip to Montana. During one of Black Foot's appearances to her, he referred to her as "my woman," and Francis Stewart later told her that that confirmed his suspicion that she had been the wife of the Chief in a previous lifetime.

She also met historian Joe Medicine Crow, who informed her that Chief Black Foot, or Sits-In-The-Middle-Of-The-Land, had been the only one ever to hold the title of chief-of-all-chiefs, and that in addition to laying the four boundaries of the reservation, he had also written the constitution and by-laws for his people. The most revealing bit of news, however, was that the Chief was believed to have been buried near Cody or Meeteetse, Wyoming.

The psychic from Virginia nearly jumped out of her skin at the sound of the name. The Chief hadn't been talking about "tsetse flies" after all!

She returned to Virginia on July 25, and the search for the Chief's remains near Meeteetse began that same week. Black Foot had told Victoria Mauricio that he would guide the party of twenty searchers through her, so there was almost constant long-distance telephone contact between the Crow Agency and Virginia Beach. One of the earliest clues relayed by the Chief came to the psychic during sleep.

"I dreamed one night that I was on top of a sandstone cliff, and I couldn't find my way back to the valley where I was born," she remembered. "I met a woman who said, 'Come to the house; we can show you how to get back to your home.' When I went to her house, she was dressed in white with an apron and she carried a basket of flowers. Six other women, identically dressed, came down a winding staircase. There were seven of the sisters, and they were all trying to give me directions.

"The dream made sense only after I realized how it fit in with another clue," the Reverend Mauricio continued. "Every time I visited a friend's house, I noticed an antique pitchfork that had been bent backwards to hold hanging baskets of flowers. The Chief kept saying to me, 'Pitchfork, pitchfork.' And I said to him, 'Yes, beautiful.' He repeated the word many times to me, even when I was in my own home, but for a long time I didn't understand what he was trying to tell me—that his remains were to be found on the Pitchfork Ranch, the heirs of which were seven sisters!"

———

She was also informed that the party of searchers were to find more than just the remains of the Chief. "One day a few weeks after returning from Montana, I came into my living room, and Black Foot said, 'I have left something for you on the small table.' It was a small blue bead, a duplicate of those which were to be found on the body. The Chief told me that when the others were found, they were to be sent to me. As soon as I passed this information on to Francis Stewart's wife, Cerise, the bead disappeared from my coffee table."

The search continued with other clues from the Chief relayed by telephone. The body was to be found in the direction of three oddly shaped rocks and a tree like a finger. The party of Crows would know they were on the right track when they heard the hooting of an owl in the daytime, and the ground near the remains would glisten. Finally, Chief Black Foot told them that they would hear an animal scratching very near the place where his bones had been laid.

On Saturday, August 26, 1978, Victoria Mauricio was awakened by the Chief's voice saying, "They will find me today at 12:15." Therefore, when Cerise Stewart called her at 3:30 P.M. eastern time, the psychic's first words were, "You've found him, haven't you?" The two women broke down and cried tears of joy. The search for the great Chief Black Foot was over at last, and the body had been discovered by Willie Plainfeather, at seventeen the youngest member of the party. According to *The Return of Chief Black Foot*, the boy was standing inside a cave and deciding to leave it when a "thing" grabbed his shoulder, then literally threw him farther into the interior of the cave. Suddenly he saw a bone sticking up through the floor of the cave, and alongside it were a buffalo hide and the beads that Chief Black Foot had promised would be there.

Cody archaeologist Bob Edgar, who had been one of the party of searchers, expressed his opinion that the remains were most likely those of the Chief, although he was puzzled as to why his wife's were not there as well. The fact that the bones had obviously belonged to a very large man made their identification with Black Foot easier— the great leader of the Crows was known to have stood at least six feet, five inches tall.

The search over, the funeral still lay ahead, and again, the Chief sent his instructions through the woman who believed herself to have been his wife in a previous life. He was to be buried on the fourth of October, and Victoria Mauricio was to be there as the honored guest of the elaborate ceremony conducted by shaman Francis Stewart.

Almost two thousand people were in attendance, including not only members of the Crow Nation, but also non-Indian Catholic priests, nuns, and Baptist ministers. Black Foot had given strict orders to be buried on a particular spot of ground near the "Indian office." He repeated the words several times, and at first it was believed that he referred to the new tribal building. But then someone remembered that in the old days, the Bureau of Indian Affairs had been called the "Indian office," and that apparently was where the Chief wanted to be laid to rest.

His choice of locale was especially interesting in view of the fact that the area turned out to be "no man's land," as Victoria Mauricio found out afterwards. Clara White Hip explained that when the section was surveyed, a little strip about the size of a house had been left out, so it now belongs neither to the B.I.A. nor to the reservation.

"That little strip belongs to no one, so no one can ever take him out of there," the Reverend Mauricio explained.

At first she thought that her mission with Chief Black Foot had ended with his funeral, but nothing could have been further from the truth. A healer since her childhood, she stayed on for a while to cure the sick on the reservation, often becoming exhausted and ill herself in the process. She also organized a clothing drive to help the Crows when a flood wiped out the personal possessions of many families, and her involvement in the Chief Black Foot story resulted in publicity on a nationwide, and occasionally even worldwide scale.

A spate of articles appeared not only in local newspapers in Virginia, Montana, and Wyoming, but also in the *National Enquirer*, *Fate*, and even the *Psychic News* in London. The story appeared as a segment of the television program, *That's Incredible*, and Victoria Mauricio was invited to appear on *P.M. Magazine* as well.

The Chief had other ideas, however. "He had let me appear on other programs with no objection, but for some reason, he didn't want me to be on this one," the Reverend Mauricio explained. "The cameras and the sound wouldn't work on the first day of filming, and for a while the Chief wouldn't tell me what was wrong. The producer said that we would try again in a few days, and the next time, the crew brought four cameras with them to my friend's house, where the program was to be taped. Again, nothing would work, although all the equipment had been carefully checked out beforehand.

"The producer thought we should go into the kitchen to make some coffee, since I was very nervous; and when I sat down in there, the Chief materialized and told me, 'You're not going to film this!' I asked why not, and he answered, 'Because Custer, the evil Yellow Hair, is here.' I had no idea what he was talking about, since I certainly couldn't see the spirit of Custer or anything. I told him so, and he told me to go tell the producer what he had just said. When I did so, the man appeared very shocked.

" 'How in the hell does he know?' he asked. It turned out that the cameraman's great great great grandmother was Custer's sister, and the cameraman was a dead ringer for 'Yellow Hair' himself!

"Another time, I was going to do a show called *Cross Talk* on WHRO-TV in Norfolk, Virginia. The host of the program told me that he had heard about the cameras failing for *P.M. Magazine* (that show was finally filmed, incidentally), and he didn't want anything like that to happen during his show. He warned the crew that if any of them were of Indian descent, they were to stay away from me, and above all, no one was to speak a word against Chief Black Foot. Well, then a black man who was the sound producer began adjusting the microphone on my chest. Apparently he hadn't heard what the host said, because as I was testing the mike, he made the mistake of telling me that his grandmother had been a full-blooded Blackfoot Indian!

"Immediately the little microphone stood up away from me in a straight line, and the host yelled for this guy to get away from me. The next thing I knew, a cameraman wheeled over a huge, brand new camera on a dolly, and said, 'What's all this baloney about blowing cameras? Nothing can happen to this one. It's computerized, and I know every inch of it. Besides, I don't believe in any of this bull, even though I'm half Cree and something else!'

"All of a sudden, there was a loud boom, and that camera had blown itself, too. The cameraman was utterly amazed, and the host almost had a heart attack. I don't know whether they ever got that camera repaired or not!"

The publicity finally abated, but Victoria Mauricio's involvement with Chief Black Foot and his beloved Crow people continued. Members of the tribe called frequently for advice from the Chief, and the psychic and healer returned to the reservation the next fall to check the progress of the patients she had helped. Unfortunately, however, her relations with the tribe eventually deteriorated, as some of the Crows denounced her as a fraud and claimed that the bones interred so elaborately during the funeral ceremony were not those of the great chief after all. Others claimed that the Crows' bad luck in politics and economics were directly traceable to the pretense that the bones were those of Black Foot, while supporters of the psychic attributed that same bad luck to the fact that she had been snubbed by some of the tribal members.

The shaman Francis Stewart remains a stalwart supporter of the Reverend Victoria Mauricio, however, still believing that her involvement with Chief Black Foot is a fulfillment of a prophecy made over one hundred years ago, that a great chief would be lost to the Crows, and that an outsider who was a healer would bring him back.

The Reverend Mauricio herself points to another charming bit of evidence that the extraordinary story of Chief Black Foot's return to his people is true. "The Chief was found on the Pitchfork Ranch near Meeteetse," she said, "and guess which animal thought to be extinct was found there since then? That's right—the blackfooted ferret!"

THE LADY
IN
GRAY

M ost people inherit material things such as houses, money, or the family silver pattern, but the members of one Wyoming family routinely inherit a ghost! For the past three hundred years, the so-called Lady in Gray has followed descendants of the Herondon family from England to Washington, D.C., to Texas to Laramie and beyond.

According to newspaper accounts in the *San Marcos [Texas] Record* and the *Laramie Boomerang*, the legend of the Lady begins with an English tea party. Young Catherine was the grandniece of Lord Herondon, and she loved nothing better than playing tricks on people. One day some visitors stopped by the family estate, and mischievous Catherine put some soap in a lady's teacup. When the lady began to grimace and sputter, Catherine broke into a fit of laughter, choked on a crumb of crumpet, and died.

The Herondons came to America in the seventeenth century and changed the spelling of their name to Herndon. They settled in Virginia on a Cavalier Grant from the English government, and since that time, the legend goes, they have passed down not only their worldly goods, but their otherworldly Catherine as well. Still a prankster, Catherine, who is always seen wearing gray, is said to appear to every other generation of the descendants of the Herndons.

Apparently the last of the Herndon line to get a good look at the Lady was Dr. Catherine Wiegand, who lived the last years of her life in Laramie. A well-respected science teacher, Dr. Wiegand understandably had a problem with the whole idea of the supernatural, but she believed that the sightings of the ghost by alternate generations of the family might result from an inherited genetic ability to see beyond the normal spectrum of light.

Her first experience with the Lady in Gray took place in San Marcos, Texas, when she was thirteen years old. As she told Vern Shelton of that city's *Record*, "The first time I saw her was about 11 A.M. one day. A lady wearing gray walked into another room and I followed her to see who she was. She just disappeared. She was dressed in long, flowing gray skirts with something gray over her head. No one has ever been able to describe her very well, since the meetings are always so unexpected. First you see her, then you don't."

When the young Catherine Herndon went to ask her mother and grandmother about the mysterious woman, they looked at each other in amazement and exclaimed, "She's seen the Lady in Gray!" That was the first time that the teenaged namesake had ever heard of Catherine's ghost, and although she apparently never saw her again, she was to have other experiences with the Lady.

When she moved to a house at 816 Mitchell in Laramie in the 1960s, for example, Dr. Wiegand soon discovered that her ghostly ancestor's favorite prank was setting off the buzzer on the kitchen stove.

As she told Robert Roten of the *Laramie Boomerang* staff, a friend had scoffed at stories of the ghost and one day marched into the kitchen and firmly turned off the buzzer. She had no sooner walked back to the living room when the buzzer sounded again. She returned to the kitchen and turned off the buzzer once more, only to have it sound another time when she reached the living room. After the process had been repeated three times, the exasperated woman hit the buzzer so hard that the glass broke. The Lady in Gray, alas, was not to be daunted so easily; for when the woman returned to the living room that time, the buzzer went off again, frightening her out the door. Needless to say, she never spoke of the ghost again!

When the family moved to another house at 1417 Bonneville, the Lady in Gray made her presence known two different times by means of a loud crashing noise in the basement. On both occasions when the Wiegands went to check, nothing had fallen down, and nothing was out of place.

While the ability to see the ghost is said to skip generations, the Lady in Gray apparently keeps tabs on all family members, including pets. Catherine Wiegand's mother once saw her cat raise its back, hiss, and then follow something invisible up a stairway, and other cats belonging to the family have reportedly had their tails pulled or stepped on by the ghost.

Another time, when Catherine was living with her uncle in Washington, D.C., a black cat in the library would often arch its back and look toward the top of the stairs. As Catherine told Vern Shelton, "I couldn't see anything, but the cat's eyes would follow something as it came downstairs and went out the door. My uncle explained it was the Lady in Gray going out for the evening."

Catherine's grandfather, Benjamin Franklin Herndon, was a Texas rancher, and reportedly *not* the type of person who believed in ghosts, but he saw the Lady in Gray when he was seventy years old. He had seen a woman walking around the house, and called to her, thinking it was his wife. When his wife answered him from another direction, he looked back to the woman he had seen, but she had already vanished. That encounter changed him immediately from a skeptic to a believer.

Catherine's granddaughter, Mary Stoll, now resides in Cedar Rapids, Iowa; but when she was growing up in Laramie, she came to take the Lady in Gray for granted. "I grew up thinking that ghosts were normal, but when I got a little older, I suddenly realized that this sort of thing doesn't happen in most other people's houses! But we had a lot of lights going on and off for no reason, and doors opening and closing, and things falling off of bookshelves and tables. And once when I was a teenager, I actually saw a doorknob turn, and the door opened, but nobody was there.

"Only one time did I come close to actually seeing the Lady in Gray. I was home alone one night, washing dishes, and I saw someone out of the corner of my eye. It was just a quick glance, but I felt that somebody was there, and I was scared, because I knew that no one else was supposed to be in the house. When I turned around again, nobody was there, so I ran and locked myself in the bathroom and didn't come out until my grandmother came home!

"I don't know why, but a lot of things used to happen when she was there. Once my friend Jerri and I had spent the night at my house, and we were talking with Grandmother in the kitchen. My friend wanted her to tell us about the Lady in Gray, but she said, 'No, she doesn't like for us to talk about her.' But Jerri kept pressing, so Grandmother began to tell the story. As soon as she did, the lights in the kitchen went off. The light switch was behind my grandmother, who was in full view of both of us. And when she reached up behind her and felt of the switch, she discovered that it had been pulled down! So it wasn't just that the lightbulb went out; somebody must have pulled the switch.

"Another time, I was visiting Jerri's house, where some mobiles were hung on the ceiling. They had been turning the same way all night, and I don't know what made me do it, but suddenly I told Jerri, 'The Lady in Gray is here now. Watch. She'll make that mobile stop.' And one of them did stop. Then I said, 'She'll make this one go the other way,' and it did go the other way. We made the mobiles stop and turn different ways just by saying that the Lady in Gray was moving them."

Now that Mary is grown, the family ghost has followed her to Cedar Rapids, delighting in the same old tricks, as well as some new ones.

"She seems to go through phases where things happen, and then they don't. But sometimes I hear someone walking around downstairs, and when I go to investigate, there's no one there. And household objects often disappear and reappear in strange places. Not long ago, my husband went to the grocery store, and he purposely took my keys with him. When he came out of the store, he reached into his pocket and pulled out *his* keys! He was very frustrated, because he knew he had taken my set. I guess the Lady in Gray was playing tricks on us the next day, too, because I had gone out, and when I got home, I reached into my pocket to pull out his keys, and there were my keys that had been missing since he thought he had them the day before! So either the Lady in Gray did that, or we're losing our minds!"

Catherine Wiegand apparently had the same trouble with the ghost's propensity for hiding things, for, as she told Robert Roten, "I think that's one reason why the Lady in Gray Legend has lasted so long. It is a very good excuse for losing things. Unfortunately, I think I am perfectly capable of losing things on my own without the help of the Lady in Gray."

Certainly the Lady can be trying at times, but those of us who didn't inherit a family ghost might well envy the descendants of the Herndons. After all, who else ever had an heirloom that was so much fun?

THE CHURCH
THAT BECAME A
HAUNTED HOUSE

Whenen Connie Snyder and Cathie Getzfried were in grade school in the early 1960s, their family—all thirteen of them—moved into what had been the old Church of the Nazarene just a couple blocks off the main street of Greybull, Wyoming. Their plan was to remodel into a private residence what had been one of the most active places of worship in the north central part of the state. For in addition to serving as a church, the building had functioned often as a kind of community center for area residents.

It didn't take the family long, however, to discover that the old church was still active—but in a way none of them had bargained for!

Granted, the high ceilings and chandeliers, the pulpit and raised stage, and the pews that looked like old theater seats lent a spooky atmosphere, as did the fifty or sixty abandoned hymn books and old Bibles scattered throughout the sanctuary upstairs.

But aside from the weird ambience of the building, more tangible manifestations began to occur. Many members of the family frequently reported feeling an unseen presence. Connie's cousin, who lived with his grandparents in their half of the structure, was

---

169

so frightened of somebody following him around that he couldn't stand being left alone there.

"It seemed to me like an overpowering observer," Connie noted. "Just as if somebody were watching every move you made, not in a vicious way, but not in a benevolent way, either. And this happened mainly upstairs, where my sister Cathie and I slept. You could also hear walking across the stage late at night, when nobody was up there."

For Connie's sister Cathie, the sounds were especially alarming, because they often seemed to precede a white mist that formed near the upstairs furnace after the two girls had retired for the night. Naturally, they were often reluctant to go upstairs to bed, and persuaded their father not to put doors on their respective bedrooms as he had planned. "That way, we could still talk back and forth and reassure each other," Cathie explained.

One night shortly after they had gone to bed, Connie heard what she thought was her sister rocking back and forth in the old wooden rocker that had been placed on the stage near the girls' sleeping quarters. "I thought she was playing a trick on me, so I whispered in a loud voice, 'You're not scaring *me*!'

"And then I heard Cathie's voice, not from the stage where I'd expected her to be, but from her bedroom. She said, 'I'm not doing anything, Connie!' I accused her again, and this time I heard the fear in her voice when she answered, 'I'm not doing it! It's rocking by itself!'

"So I got up and saw that she was in her bedroom; then I looked out at the stage. It seemed like an eternity that I watched that chair rock back and forth with no one in it, but I know it was only a few seconds. It went real fast, then slow, just like somebody was actually sitting in it and rocking rhythmically."

Connie insists that there is no logical explanation for what she saw and heard. "It was airtight upstairs, so there were no breezes, and that stage was hardwood," she said. "The whole upstairs was hardwood, and constructed so well that there were no vibrations. The floor didn't even creak when someone walked across it."

Terrified by the experience, the girls screamed and ran downstairs, where they slept on the couch that night. "And the next day," Connie remembered, "I turned that chair upside down, and it stayed like that until I moved away from home."

On another occasion when Cathie was sleeping in one of the upstairs bedrooms, she watched in fascination as some curtains hanging in the doorway between the stage and her room began to move, even though there was absolutely no breeze.

Other displays of psychic phenomena were witnessed by the entire family. "You could smell flowers throughout the house, as if somebody were spraying floral scents all over the place," Connie recalled. "This usually occurred toward the beginning of the year, and the smell would fade away after a couple of weeks. No one could ever figure it out, because we never brought flowers into the house. And we didn't use air fresheners, perfumes, or scented cosmetics of any kind. So if you smelled flowers in the house, you wondered where the aroma was coming from. It smelled like roses to me. Sometimes lilacs, but mostly roses."

Often accompanying the mysterious fragrance were the equally puzzling sounds of a baby crying and organ music. "Lots of times you'd smell the roses and then you'd hear a baby crying, but it seemed like the baby was a long way off," Connie said. "The sound came from somewhere within the house, but there was no baby in our home. I had some little sisters at the time, but they weren't infants. I would even check outside, but there was never any kid there, either. In fact, when you went outside, you could tell that the sound was definitely coming from the inside of the house.

"I must have heard the baby crying ten or fifteen times at least. It wasn't a loud cry, but it would last maybe ten minutes. And then you would hear it again a few days later.

"My grandmother loved babies, and she was always hearing the sound. She came over to our side of the building one day and asked, 'Who has brought a baby down here? I'm *sure* I just heard one crying through the wall.'

"My mother said, 'No, it's *that* baby again.' And then they looked strangely at each other and quickly changed the subject. Most of the time, though, we learned to take all these things in stride. We thought some of the phenomena might have been left over from weddings, funerals, christenings, or other occasions observed in the church."

The organ music was also believed to have been a psychic legacy of the church in its heyday, and it was often heard at the same time as the baby's cry. Cathie remembers that the tune was always the same, but it wasn't one she could identify. "It didn't last very long, and then you'd hear this faint sound of the baby crying, and then it would all go away. And then in two or three days, you'd hear it again.

"And just like with the smell of flowers, these sounds were seasonal, occurring only about a month out of the year. I can't remember when it was exactly, but I do remember it always took place during cold weather," Cathie pointed out.

"And of course there was no longer an organ in the building, but the strange thing was that when you sat on the edge of the stage upstairs, the music was louder than when you were in the bedrooms. It sounded like it was coming from the same room, but it was very faint. It didn't sound muffled, but instead as if someone were playing very lightly, as if the volume had been turned way down. And you couldn't hear it at all downstairs."

For Cathie, the ghostly organ music was the eeriest experience of all. "There was nothing you could do about it," she explained. "Connie and I would be lying in bed at night, and very faintly we would hear the strains of this music. You'd cover up your head with the bedclothes, but you could still hear it. It sounded like funeral music.

"Connie and I were so scared that once when Mom and Dad were out, we tore up part of the stage, trying to figure out where the sound might be coming from. We wondered if maybe there were a baby buried there, but of course we never found anything."

As Cathie's father continued to remodel the house, fewer and fewer peculiar things occurred, leading Cathie to wonder whether the changes to the structure were somehow destroying any psychic imprints that had been recorded into the physical environment of the building. The organ music, however, continued to be heard, even by those outside the family.

"Some friends of ours didn't believe us when we told them about it, so Connie and I invited them home, and they heard it," Cathie said.

The unearthly occurrences were apparently even more terrifying to the animals in the house than they were to the humans. The worst experience concerned a kitten belonging to Connie, who was literally frightened to death by something that no one else could sense.

"I had just come in from school, and the cat suddenly seemed to be hurled down the stairs, just as if someone had thrown it," Connie recalled. "It bounced off the wooden steps and flopped onto the floor. At first we thought it had been poisoned or had simply gone berserk, because its eyes were crazy and wild-looking. And then it seemed to be picked up again and thrown inside the door. Then it rolled down those stairs and plopped into an open drawer. I was afraid to look inside, because I thought maybe the cat had distemper."

But it was just lying there, its chest briskly heaving up and down and its eyes frenzied and hysterical. Connie watched in horror as the kitten gasped its last breath.

"We took it to the vet for an autopsy, and he said that it hadn't been poisoned, but that it had evidently been so scared that its blood pressure shot up, causing its heart to explode, as it would in a massive heart attack. But I just couldn't figure out what had scared it so much. It had been perfectly okay when I went to school that morning."

Several years later, after she was grown, Connie moved out. But in 1974 she moved back for about six months. During that time the two cats who lived with her also seemed to be frequently aware of an unsettling presence in the house.

"They would make that throaty growl and stare at the ceiling, twisting their heads around," Connie said. "They could see something, but I couldn't. Their fur would raise up, and when they looked at me, I could see anger and fear in their eyes. The way they acted really gave me the creeps."

Connie's parents eventually sold the house, and it was converted into an apartment building. Cathie Getzfried reported that some of the new residents had told her that their apartment was always cold, and Connie Snyder met another inhabitant who would say only that she had lived there for two months, but couldn't take the weird place and moved out.

Is it possible, then, that this old church from the early years of the century could have retained impressions from its past? And if so, did the renovating undergone by Connie and Cathie's family release those impressions and subsequently put an end to most of them, as more and more of the original structure was altered?

Whatever the truth about the old church, it made believers in the supernatural out of many of those who lived there. Cathie Getzfried summed up her experience by confessing, "Sometimes even now, in the night, I think back to that place and it still gives me an eerie feeling. I always thought ghosts belonged only in fairy tales, but after living in that house, I would swear that there are such things as ghosts! I can swear up and down there are!"

THE SHOSHONE BAR IS HAUNTED!

P erhaps the rumor that a body lies buried in the basement is to blame, but patrons and employees alike have known for a long time that there's something just a mite peculiar about the Shoshone Bar in Lovell. The sighting of apparitions and the hearing of unexplained noises, as well as the weird malfunctioning of electrical devices, have made the bar the one place *not* to be alone, especially at night.

Over fifty years old, the drinking establishment on the main street of this largely Mormon community has nevertheless become a sort of fixture of the town; and in spite of various alterations to its physical structure and the change of personnel over the years, the Shoshone Bar still seems to harbor two ghosts, that of a former owner and that of a man whose disappearance is to this day one of the biggest unsolved mysteries in the state of Wyoming.

The story of Ted Louie's vanishing would make for a fascinating read even without the ghost story associated with it. For few people have managed to drop off the face of the earth as utterly without a trace as the easygoing sweets and cigarette vendor whose job earned him the nickname the "Candy Man."

A resident of Thermopolis, Ted Louie was well past middle age at the time of his disappearance. Aside from the fact that he sometimes drank too much and flashed his money around (when he had it), Ted was apparently just an average guy, generally well liked, with no known enemies. His trademark was the Stetson hat with a silver band that he often wore, and his job delivering vending machine products to various outlets made him familiar to people all over the Bighorn Basin.

On an autumn day in the late 1940s, Ted arrived in Lovell, not in his customary van, but by bus. The owner of the Shoshone Bar at the time was Buell Scherck, and he clearly remembers the day before Ted vanished.

"He must have gotten into town around four o'clock, and when I came to work at six," Buell recalled, "he was sitting at the end of the bar. I asked him what he was doing in town, and he said that he wasn't here on business, but had just come for a visit. He sat there and had a couple of drinks, then left to have supper at the cafe next door.

"He came back to the Shoshone afterwards, and sat at the end of the bar until closing time at midnight. Oddly enough, he didn't order even a single drink after he'd had supper, and he seemed very far away and preoccupied, not like himself at all. Two or three times I asked him, 'Ted, do you feel all right?' but he kept insisting that he was fine.

"When I locked up the place at twelve, I asked him where he was staying, and he told me at the Shoshone Hotel, which was just half a block away. My wife and I offered to give him a lift, and before we left the bar, Ted said, 'Hey, maybe you'd better cash a check for me for ten dollars.' I took his check and gave him the money; that was the last check ever to clear his bank account. We drove him to his hotel, double parked in front of it, and Ted got out of the car. My wife and I both saw him walk through the doors of the building, and we could see a light on inside.

"The next morning I went to check on things at work, and I asked the bartender if Ted had been in yet. He said no, and I went over to the cafe next door for a cup of coffee, but the waitress there hadn't seen him, either. As that day and then the next wore on, Ted never showed up, and his sister in Thermopolis finally called to ask where he was.

"Search parties of kids as well as adults started looking for him all over town and along the highway as far as Frannie and Powell," Buell continued, "and a friend and I floated the Shoshone River on a rubber raft. I even checked at the depot to see whether he'd taken a bus out of town, but no one remembered him doing so. In fact, nobody had the faintest idea about what had happened to Ted after my wife and I dropped him off at the Shoshone Hotel."

The front desk clerk on duty that night told several people that she remembered hearing Ted Louie talking to someone in the entryway, but she never saw him come on into the lobby. To whom he was speaking or what happened after he left the hotel again is anyone's guess, but the woman who cleaned up the Shoshone Bar after closing told Buell Scherck that around one o'clock that same morning, she heard somebody knocking on the front door.

"She was too frightened to let anyone in, but she said that she looked up from her work to see a fellow wearing a white Stetson hat. She didn't get a good look, but she presumed that it was Ted Louie," Buell said. "And there was a later report that someone dressed like Ted was seen getting into a car, but that was never verified."

There are only a few theories about what happened to the Candy Man, and of those few, not a shred of evidence exists to back up any of them. Most people in Lovell today think that Ted, who bought and sold cattle as a sideline business, was killed for the large amounts of money he was often believed to carry. On the night he disappeared, however, he apparently had on his person only the ten dollars he had gotten from Buell Scherck; but his killer wouldn't necessarily have known that.

If Ted was murdered, though, or for that matter, if he died in any other way, why was his body never found?

Buell Scherck's theory is that Ted might have gone wandering off into the countryside to meet with some kind of natural disaster, but his speculation about the location of the remains would also be a possibility if Ted was murdered.

"I think his body is probably still out in some gully," Buell explained. "Years ago, there used to be a refinery with a lot of pits filled with crude oil that were covered up with dirt. At the time Ted disappeared, you could walk right across most of them, but he might have fallen into one."

Or, presumably, his body might have been dropped into one. This theory would also explain why no one has ever found his trademark Stetson with its band of silver that would tarnish but not decompose. A similar theory is that the body might have been buried in a sinkhole up in the Bighorn Mountains.

Whatever happened to Ted, it must have occurred right after the Schercks deposited him at the hotel, because he never spent the night there. The person with whom he spoke in the entryway must have been somehow involved in his disappearance, so abduction followed by murder seems a likely possibility.

Two other theories about Ted's fate seem less plausible. The first, that he staged his own disappearance, is weak because he had no known motive or means for doing so. The second, that he crawled into the back seat of a stranger's car and fell asleep or perhaps even died after having too much to drink, is not borne out by what little evidence there is. Bob Bischoff pointed out that Ted often used to sleep in cars when he was drunk, but according to Buell Scherck, the Candy Man had had no alcohol for several hours when he returned to his hotel. The possibility exists that he could have left again and gotten drunk with the mysterious person with whom he spoke in the entryway, and *then* have fallen asleep in a car; but it seems unlikely that the driver of any such vehicle would have harmed Ted. If the Candy Man was found dead, however, the driver might have panicked and disposed of his body in one of the ways mentioned previously.

The investigation of the disappearance continued for several months without one real clue turning up. Even the FBI became involved, owing to the possibility that Ted might have been abducted across state lines.

"I must have talked to their agents a dozen times," Buell Scherck recalled, "but even after I had sold the bar and moved to Worland, they still weren't finished with me. One night my former bartender, Myron Durtche, called me and said, 'You'll never guess what's happened now. The cops think you killed Ted Louie and buried him in the basement!'"

That the police had come in with floodlights and jackhammers to dig up the cellar of the Shoshone was bad enough, but what their excavation revealed was even worse.

"The basement was sort of a dugout with a dirt floor on one side," Buell explained, "and one year Myron and I had killed an elk a little bit out of season. We took it to the basement and hung it in the walk-in beer cooler; then we butchered it and buried the bones underneath the floor. Well, you can imagine what the policemen and FBI agents thought when they found those bones! They sent them off to determine whether they were human, but of course they weren't. I can laugh about the whole thing now, but back then it didn't seem so funny!"

Although none but elk bones were found buried in the basement of the Shoshone Bar, many of its employees, including some who didn't even know the story of the Candy Man, have been frightened to go down there. The ghostly activity was apparently so intense that it occasionally spilled over into Dude's Restaurant next door, which could be entered directly from the bar, and which from time to time even had the same owners. One of the dishwashers there claimed to have conversed with a presence who had traveled from the basement of the bar to that of the restaurant; and after her ordeal, she refused to set foot downstairs again.

Has the spirit of Ted Louie been responsible all these years for haunting the Shoshone Bar and its environs? While apparitions have been seen from time to time, none has been positively identified as his, although that may be explained simply by the fact that those witnessing the phenomena never knew the Candy Man and therefore wouldn't recognize him.

Sherri Phillips worked at Dude's Restaurant off and on from 1979 to 1983, and she'll never forget an incident that took place one night after closing.

"I locked the door and put the money away, and the other waitresses and I, all teenagers, went out and got in my car to go drag Main," Sherri recalled. "I looked back at the restaurant and thought I saw somebody standing inside, leaning with his arm against the counter where the hot food waits to be picked up. He was dressed all in black, including his hat. I didn't say anything, but when I saw the other girls with their mouths hanging open, I could tell that they had seen the same thing.

"At first we thought that we must have accidentally locked somebody in there. After all, the man could have been in the bathroom when we closed up. We went to the police to explain what we thought had happened, and they searched the whole building but didn't find anybody.

"Naturally, after that, we were the laughing stock of the whole town," Sherri admitted. "But all three of us saw that man in there, and we really thought we had locked him in."

Dave and Verna Hayward owned Dude's from 1977 to 1982, and Dave repeatedly saw something out of the corners of his eyes.

"I'd see something flash by heading toward the bathroom, but by the time I turned around to look, it was always gone," he said. "It didn't really look like a man—it was more like a white puff of smoke, except that it had more shape to it. I often followed it into the bathroom, where I would get a weird chill, but I couldn't see anything. This happened to me probably thirty to forty times, usually just before closing, when I was alone in the place. As a result, I started believing in ghosts.

"Only once did I see more than just a flash, and that time I noticed what seemed to be a man's back," he explained. "It looked real, except that it had no color. It was just white."

Jerry Hayes, who with his wife Joyce owned the Shoshone Bar several years later, remembered the time that one of his female customers got more than just a sideways glance at the phantom.

"I was at the bar when this gal came running out of the women's restroom," he said, "screaming that she had just seen a man in there. I went to check, but of course, the room was empty."

Whether Ted Louie haunted the Shoshone Bar or not, it seems clear that he wasn't (and still isn't) the only ghost on the premises. Upon several occasions, former owner Allan Grant* has apparently paid a phantom visit to his old stomping grounds.

"Before we bought this place, there were big picture windows facing the street," Jerry Hayes recalled. "People used to go by at night after everything was closed, when all the chairs were left upside down on the tables and all the ashtrays were cleaned and put away; and they'd see somebody sitting in there at a table, smoking a cigarette. Several times, the police were alerted, but they were never able to find more than the chair pulled up to the table and a used ashtray. Whoever had enjoyed that solitary smoke was gone.

"I never gave much thought to that story until one night when I was alone in the bar after closing," Jerry continued. "I was counting money out of the number one cash register, when I turned around slightly and caught a glimpse of a guy sitting at the bar right behind me! He had on a plaid shirt and a funny little knitted cap, and he didn't say a word—he just stared at me. But when I lunged around, startled, to get a better look, he disappeared!

"Seeing him like that really shook me up, because he looked absolutely real. There was no doubt in my mind that someone was sitting there, and I can see him in my mind's eye even now."

Jerry had no idea whose ghost it was, however, until he spoke with some of the bar's patrons about a similar experience they had had.

"Three of the four persons involved told me his or her account at a different time, each one said exactly the same thing, and they all insisted that they were sober at the time," Jerry said. "One night they were in the Shoshone, two of them standing at the end of the bar and the other two sitting. One of the men said he looked up suddenly and saw Allan Grant, a former owner of the bar who had been dead for some time!

"The ghost was standing there just as big as life, right in front of the women's restroom, where the carpet ends and the dance floor begins. The man kept staring in disbelief, until he finally nudged his wife, who turned around and saw the phantom, too. By that time, all four people were staring at their long-deceased friend, and finally the first man called out, 'Allan!' With that, the ghost reached up, graciously tipped his cap, then strolled into the women's lavatory! One of the watchers followed him in, but nobody was there."

Because of the detail of the knitted hat, Jerry believes that the phantom he saw was also probably that of Allan Grant, who was rarely seen without his stocking cap, even when tending bar.

While many of the psychic phenomena experienced over the years haven't involved apparitions, they have certainly been just as alarming. The former owner of Dude's, Verna Hayward, often heard the sounds of footsteps and chairs bumping around in the still-darkened dining room while she prepared food in the kitchen, and waitresses frequently heard footsteps going up the stairs into the bosses' office, followed by the sound of the door opening and closing, even though it was always kept locked.

Joyce Hayes once heard the tumblers turning on the old-fashioned safe up in the front of the Shoshone Bar. "I was alone in the building, cleaning the women's bathroom, and I expected our bartender, Sue Knop, to be coming to work shortly," she explained. "When I heard the tumblers twisting around, I thought maybe Sue had come in without my knowing, so I hollered out her name but got no answer. I stepped out of the bathroom to see who had been playing with the safe, and I saw that I was still alone. I'm really not one to believe in ghosts, but I can't explain what happened."

Another time, Joyce and her husband Jerry were locking up after a busy night when they heard a commotion in the basement. "It sounded like lots of boxes were falling all over the place," Jerry said, "and Joyce thought that somebody had been hiding down there to rob the bar after we left. I grabbed a club and went down the stairs, but there was not a thing out of place and not a soul was there. In fact, there were only a few boxes in the basement, not nearly enough to make the sound that we had heard, like tall stacks of empty ones knocking into each other.

"On another occasion, when the safety bar on our back entrance had disappeared so that there was no way to lock the door, I ended up spending the night in the building," Jerry continued. "Joyce brought me a sleeping bag and a quilt for padding, and I also got a .38 from my office. I undressed, got into the sleeping bag, and laid the gun right by my head. The bar was locked up tight, except for the back door, and near there was where I was going to sleep.

"I was just about to doze off when I heard the tumblers in the front door turning," Jerry said. "I heard somebody inserting a key; then I heard the door unlocking before it opened and closed again. Then, just as sure as anything, I heard footsteps coming down the length of the bar.

"I was fully awake and scared now, because nobody was supposed to be in that place but me. I jumped up and grabbed my gun; but as I ran around in my shorts and waved that pistol in the air, I saw that I *was* alone. Not only that—when I went to check the front door, it was still locked!

"Another time when I was closing up the bar," Jerry continued, "I heard the unmistakable sound of somebody knocking three times in quick succession from the restaurant side of the door. I thought it might have been someone who had gotten drunk and passed out, only to wake up later to find himself locked in. I went into Dude's and searched every square inch of that place, including the basement, but I found no one. I can't explain where the noise came from, because none of the businesses surrounding the bar and restaurant should have had anyone on their premises at night."

Sherri Phillips and other waitresses at Dude's also heard loud banging noises, as well as the shrill notes of a more musically inclined phantom. "It sounded as if a man were standing in the front dining room whistling, and I think it was always the same tune," she said. "And once when we were cleaning up the kitchen, we heard a big bus tub loaded with dishes slam down in the dining room. But when we went to look, there wasn't any bus tub back there!"

One of the strangest phenomena was encountered by former bartender Sue Knop at the Shoshone. "One day a customer came in, ordered a drink, and laid a five dollar bill on the bar," she explained. "As he did that, I set his drink down; then we both watched in amazement as the money suddenly rose up an inch and a half into the air and floated three feet down the length of the bar! I told that man, 'You're not leaving! You're staying right here, because I don't want to be alone in this place!'

"At first I thought that an air current might have picked up the money," Sue said. "But this happened in the early fall, when we didn't have any heat on, and no doors were open."

Even more perplexing is the story of Bobbie Pulley, who discovered evidence of a ghostly tippler who made himself at home during the Shoshone's after hours.

"We closed the bar at two o'clock," she explained, "and we cleared away all the glasses and ashtrays as usual. But when I came back to open again at six, a glass was sitting on the bar with a few drops of whiskey in it. I knew darn well that it hadn't been there when I left!"

The whiskey-drinking ghost sounds suspiciously like the solitary smoker described earlier, but who is to blame for the erratic behavior of certain electrical devices in the bar?

Sue Knop and her mother, Dorothy Eidum, were alone in the establishment one morning when the jukebox suddenly began to play. "There was no one even near it," Dorothy insisted, "and nobody had put in any money, and there's no way you can turn on the jukebox from behind the bar. I asked Sue what in the world was going on, and she said, 'Oh, it's that ghost from downstairs!' "

Many others also experienced the jukebox turning itself on, and Joyce Hayes often joked that the ghost had strange taste in music, because he usually picked songs that no one else liked. "And sometimes the channels on the television would change by themselves, too," she added, "but I always thought that somebody outside might have had a remote control or some other kind of gadget that could have caused that to happen."

Less easy to rationalize, perhaps, is the unnerving experience Bobbie Pulley had with some lights over the bandstand. "One Saturday night after closing, I had just put the money in the bag and was ready to leave, when my husband phoned me," she recalled. "In the middle of our conversation, those lights suddenly came on and scared me half to death. I hollered, then told my husband what had happened, and he asked me who else was in the building. I assured him that I was all alone. To turn those lights off meant going up onto the stage, and I was not about to do that! So I just left them on, put the bag of money in the deep freeze, and got out of there as soon as I could!"

Jerry Hayes was another who had a strange experience with the bandstand lights. "A panel of switches on the wall controls them," he explained, "and I had turned off one switch, but the light stayed on, anyway. I double checked to make sure that I had flipped the switch, and I had. So I flipped it back and forth again to the off position, but the light remained on even so. Deciding that there was a short somewhere, I started walking away. But when I turned around to look again, the light was off!"

Next, Jerry checked to make sure that the lights and switches were all properly connected, and he moved the switch back and forth until everything appeared to be working normally. "I left the switch in the off position and started walking away," he said, "but when I looked up at the light again, it flashed on and off at me!"

The various unexplained happenings at the Shoshone Bar have caused many a skeptic to reconsider the subject of the supernatural. Jerry Hayes, for example, never believed in ghosts before he bought the bar, but now he admits that he can't explain away the weird things he experienced there.

"I swear to you, my right hand raised to God, that those are true stories I've told you," Jerry said. "There might be a perfectly logical explanation, but I don't know what it would be. All I *do* know is that if there are ghosts at the Shoshone, they've never hurt anybody and we've actually had lots of fun with them. We used to have costume parties every Halloween, and once we decorated the basement by putting a tombstone over where the floor had been dug up. On it we wrote, 'Rest in Peace, Fred Leroy,' since that sounded like Ted Louie's name. Then we had a full man-sized dummy with a lifelike head made up, and we laid it out in a casket. Halloween was always one of our biggest nights!"

That seems only fitting for what is surely Wyoming's most haunted bar. And since they have always been so clearly appreciated by the patrons and employees, whatever ghosts may be there would probably do well just to stick around.

APPENDIX
Additional Readings

Tom Bishop, "Wyoming Ghost Stories: A Collection of Campfire Tales," *Wyoming Horizons*, April 1985. This roundup contains four early stories, the first about the Lone Scout who was killed by Indians as he rode to warn his fellow soldiers of an uprising among the tribes. This phantom was originally reported to WPA interviewer Alice C. Guyol of Hartville, Wyoming, by "the man who saw the apparition" near Cheyenne. Bishop's second campfire tale involves two sheep ranchers, Vedder and Koch, who argued over grazing range in 1895. Koch killed Vedder, whose ghost supposedly still visits the area around Douglas. Bishop's third story is about the ghost of a miner from the Black Hills who was tortured and murdered by ruffians seeking his gold, and the fourth campfire tale concerns the specter of a Chinese miner who was massacred, along with many of his compatriots, by a white mob. Always thereafter, the presence of the Chinese ghost foretold disaster in the mines around Rock Springs.

Vincent H. Gaddis, "Wyoming's Ship of Death," *Fate*, 1 (Spring 1948). While it seems unlikely that a state as dry as Wyoming would have its own ghostly sailing vessel, legend holds that just such a ship has appeared from time to time in various places along the Platte River. To see the phantom craft is always bad luck, for it is an omen of death. According to the Cheyenne Bureau of Psychological Research, the ship first appeared in 1862 to Leon Webber, an Indian Scout, who saw a vision of the corpse of his fiancee aboard. A month later, he learned that she had died the same afternoon he had had the eerie experience. The ship was sighted again in 1887 and 1903, and on both of these occasions, it also foretold death.

Kit Collings, "The Women Who Haunt the Fort," *True West*, August 1987. This article tells the legends of the Lady in Green and Brings Water, both of whom are also dealt with in my chapter "The Past Never Dies at Fort Laramie."

Wyoming Writers Program, *Wyoming: A Guide to Its History, Highways, and People* (New York: Oxford University, 1941), 122–23. In the chapter titled "Folklore and Folkways," the following paragraph appears:

> Throughout the Rocky Mountain and Plains region, and especially in Wyoming, ghosts and restless spirits are rare. A few phantom riders have been known, especially where unexplained killings have occurred. Above one famous hot spring in the Big Horn Basin a pale man on a white horse floats in the mist. Ghost lights appear in a small area south of Newcastle on the old Morrisey Road; some say they emanate as fox fire from the soil. There are haunted tunnels on the old Cross Anchor Ranch where murders were once committed. Here at night moans and groans and angry voices rise above the rustle of shuffled cards and the clack of poker chips.

Charles C. Stemmer, "Animals Live in Spirit Too," *Fate*, 13 (December 1960). This account contains several stories of animals whose spirits apparently survived death. One tale, set on Horse Creek north of Cheyenne, concerns a ghost cat who repeatedly let himself into a house by opening the screen door.

Norma Trout, "The Powder River Ghost," *Fate*, 22 (February 1969). This story, set in a sod house in northeastern Wyoming in the early 1900s, describes the visit of Earl van Cleft to his sister-in-law Laura Christine Moore. Only after he left did Laura discover that she had been called on by a ghost—at the time she saw him, Earl had already committed suicide because his wife was involved with another man.

Tom Rousseau, "I Saw the Spirit of all Animal Life," *Fate*, 14 (September 1961). This article recounts the time that the author and Chief Plentyclothes of the Crow Indians saw a giant silver tip grizzly that the chief referred to as "the spirit of all animal life." The phantom left no tracks on the ground, but its claw marks measured fourteen feet up from the base of a pine tree.

Danton Walker, "Stuart Cloete's Story," *Spooks Deluxe* (New York: Franklin Watts, 1956). In this chapter, writer Stuart Cloete tells of an uncanny experience at the Jackson Hole ranch of Struthers Burt.

A group of people were sitting around a campfire when they heard and felt the vibrating hoofbeats of an invisible horse.

John "Ace" Bonar, "Ghosts Come in Glass Bottles," *Pride, Power, Progress: Wyoming's First 100 Years* (Casper, Wyoming: Wyoming Historical Press, 1987). Unquestionably the weirdest house in the state is described in this chapter. Harry Widholm spent ten years collecting 35,000 formaldehyde bottles from mortuaries throughout the West, and he used them to construct Crystal Castle near Buford, Wyoming, in the early 1960s. Observers have noticed strange lights and shadows inside the house when it was supposed to be empty.

Earl Murray, *Ghosts of the Old West* (Chicago: Contemporary Books, 1988). This fine collection of stories includes two chapters about Wyoming ghosts, "The Phantoms of Fort Laramie," and "The Ghost in the Sheridan Inn." The latter tells the story of the phantom of Miss Kate Arnold, a housekeeper who worked at the inn for sixty-five years, and who loved it so much that after death, she was given her own private room, and her ashes were buried in the wall.

INDEX